In Joy!

Memoir of an amazingly-healed, delightfully-free, prophetic artist

Camille Riggs

In Joy! Memoir of an amazingly-healed, delightfully-free, prophetic artist
Camille Riggs
Copyright 2017 Camille Riggs

Scripture citations marked AMP are taken from the *Amplified New Testament*, copyright 1954,1958,1987 by the Lockman Foundation. All rights reserved.

Scripture citations marked BEREAN are taken from the *Berean Study Bible*, copyright 2016 by Bible Hub Publishing. All rights reserved.

Scripture citations marked ESV are taken from the *Holy Bible English Standard Version*. Copyright 2001 by Crossway. All rights reserved.

Scripture citations marked NIV are taken from the *Holy Bible New International Version*. Copyright 1973,1978,1984,2011 by Biblica, Inc. All rights reserved.

Front Cover: "Falling into Grace," acrylic, Camille Riggs, artist
Back Cover: "Healed, Delivered, Set Free," self-portrait, watercolor, Camille Riggs, artist

All rights reserved. No portion of this publication may be reproduced, stored in a retrieval system, or transmitted in any form by any means – electronic, mechanical, photocopying, recording, or any other – without prior permission from the author.

Printed in the United States of America.

www.injoypaintings.com

TABLE OF CONTENTS

Chapter 1:	AN UNEXPECTED ENCOUNTER	1
Chapter 2:	AT THE MERCY OF PAIN	11
Chapter 3:	DIVINE SET UP	19
Chapter 4:	MIRACLE IN THE MAKING	29
Chapter 5:	FOREVER CHANGED	39
Chapter 6:	FROM WHITE SPACE TO WORSHIP	47
Chapter 7:	FINDING FREEDOM	59
Chapter 8:	PARADIGM SHIFT	71
Chapter 9:	SPIRIT-EMPOWERED LIVING	81
Chapter 10:	TAPPING INTO POWER	89
Chapter 11:	DISCOVERING ME	99
Chapter 12:	PAINTING HIS VOICE	109
Chapter 13:	CALL TO DREAM	117
Chapter 14:	YOU ARE TREASURE!	123
	IMPASSIONED STORIES	127
	RESOURCES	156
	END NOTES	158

CHAPTER 1:

AN UNEXPECTED ENCOUNTER

MEETING LEE

"That was the strangest encounter I've ever had. Did you see that guy?" My business partner looked at me with an expression on her face that said, "Are you serious? Look at all the people here," as another customer came up and drew her attention away. I went back to my painting table and tried to re-focus my thoughts.

Thirty minutes before I had been contentedly painting at my art table, enjoying the many interruptions of customers, buyers, and fellow entrepreneurs who would stop to watch me paint, inquire about our products, or place an order. It was a festive, active environment on this day, the first of the four-day January Gift Market at the Dallas Trade Center. The atmosphere was charged with the elixir of every entrepreneur's dream – the anticipation of successful commerce.

The first day always sets the pace of a trade show, and it's a time to savor. Months of product preparation, marketing strategies, and catalog development are behind you. More importantly, the sweat equity of setting up your booth has been expended and you find yourself ready to interact with the public – hopefully, the buying public. Personally, as a watercolor artist, I like to demonstrate my painting techniques to whomever passes by. It draws them in and gives us a starting point for interaction. This was the case when Lee stepped into my booth – or so I thought. In truth, as I would later learn, I did not draw him in. He was sent to me.

His husky, yet gentle, voice engaged me in conversation as my head was inclined over my painting. I completed a few time-sensitive brush strokes before lifting my head. There before me stood a man in his early thirties whom I would have probably been hesitant to engage with had we not been in this particular environment. Immediately, my eyes were drawn to the black, earlobe-stretching, gauged earrings that were a stark contrast against the paleness of his skin, equaled by the dark color of his hair, cut short at the temples and combed toward his forehead. He wore around his neck a lanyard that indicated his status as a fellow entrepreneur, and I noticed colorful tattoos peeking out from under his more conventional, button-down shirt sleeves. "This is going to be interesting," I thought to myself.

We made our introductions, and I learned that Lee was hosting a booth for a web-development company on one of the lower floors. As I recall, we were talking about my art when Lee abruptly jolted the conversation into another direction as he stated very matter-of-factly, "You're in pain." I was, indeed, but how did he know that? I was sitting down, my cane was hidden away out of sight, my TENS[1] unit (a medical device used to manage chronic pain) was concealed beneath my clothing, and I was perplexed at his declaration. I sloughed it off dismissively, as was my custom, "Oh, it's chronic, and I'm used to it. Nothing to be concerned about," and attempted to redirect the conversation. No luck there. "The pain is in your lower back," he continued while gesturing with his hand to his lower back. "It's traveling down your right leg toward your knee," he said as he extended his hand in the exact path of the pain I was feeling.

I was shocked. My chronic pain that day was both intense and increasing due to a pinched sciatic nerve. In spite of the pain (and my better judgment), I had made the decision that morning to attend the trade show, asking the Lord for the strength to do it. At the very moment that Lee had interrupted my painting, he had also interrupted my thoughts of giving in to the pain and going home. Yes, the pain was intense, but the thought of maneuvering through the crowds of people, being jostled in an over-crowded elevator, traversing a Texas-size building lobby, enduring the shuttle bus ride, and sitting in snail-paced traffic was equally daunting. I was trying to come to grips with the fact that, at least for the moment, I was stuck. Then along came Lee to state the obvious, "You're in pain."

How did he know that? And why did he feel the need to remind me of it? It was not unusual for my family and close friends to be able to interpret my level of pain from the weariness in my eyes or my encumbered gait, but this guy was a total stranger – and a strange one, at that! For eighteen years I had practiced the art of keeping my pain to myself. I was pretty skilled at it, too – never wanting my pain to define me.

As I was processing this curiously-odd person who had just made this seemingly-random, yet accurate, declaration, he abruptly changed the subject, "Tell me about your two dogs?" What??!!

Now he was no longer curiously odd. He was just odd! How on earth does he know I have two dogs? Stranger-danger warnings began to go off in my head. He leaned forward a bit, looked more intently into my eyes, and said again with slow, gentle reassurance, "Tell me about your two dogs."

Something melted inside me for that brief moment, and I found myself describing Gracie and Stella, both toy-size Australian Shepherds. "Gracie is loyal and gentle, only wanting to sit in your lap and have you love on her. Stella, on the other hand, is joyful, playful, abounding in energy and always wanting more attention than you could ever possibly give her." I caught myself, thinking, "Why am I telling this to a total stranger, especially one who might turn out to be my personal stalker?" I tried again to re-direct the conversation – or better, yet, end it – but he carried on.

"I'm a believer in Jesus Christ," he said.

In an uncharacteristically unguarded response, I blurted out, "I love

Jesus, too."

"I know," he continued. "Sometimes God tells me things about people. It's called a "word of knowledge." He told me you were in pain and had two dogs, and he wants you to know that he sees you in the very way that you just described Gracie and Stella. You have both a loving, gentle side to your personality and an exuberant, joyful side. God loves that about you! Would it be OK if I prayed for you?"

Personally, I love prayer and was happy to have him pray for me. I wasn't too sure about his theology, but I applauded his exuberance and boldness. He put his hand on my shoulder and began to pray, asking the Lord to heal me. Honestly? I thought it was a sweet gesture, but I was skeptical. I had been prayed for many times over the past two decades with little result. Why would this be any different?

I thanked him for his prayers. Before turning to leave, he said confidently, "God is going to heal you, so don't be surprised if you wake up pain-free tomorrow."

"OK. Thanks!" came out of my mouth with a smile, but inside my head an uncharacteristically sarcastic response was being played out: "Yea, right. You're just one of *those* Christians who live on a cloud and thinks the world is full of rainbows or whatever else you have tattooed on your body. You have no idea what kind of pain I live with and no two-minute prayer is going to make it go away."

Although his prayer seemed to me a sweet but naive gesture, there was something profound about that encounter that both touched me and left me feeling unsettled.

HEALING OIL OR LIVING WATER?

I cannot remember a time in my life when I didn't love Jesus. I gave my heart to Him when I was eight years old and never looked back. Life without the love of God is unimaginable to me, both then and now. But I was raised in the heart of the Bible Belt where Evangelical Protestantism[2] is accepted as the norm as long it remains conservative and predictable.

Jesus healed people back in the Bible days, right? He cast out demons, raised people from the dead, foretold the future, and gave the apostles the authority to do all that stuff, too. He gave them these amazing spiritual gifts, like the working of miracles and the gift of faith, so they could do a better job of showing people what Jesus is like. He even gave them a special language, the gift of tongues, so they could better communicate with God. [3]

But as a conservative Evangelical, I had learned from childhood that, as amazing as these gifts were, they were only available to the apostles who knew and walked with Jesus personally. Once the apostles died, so did the gifts. They call it "cessationism"[4] theology because they believe the practice of the gifts have ceased. It was what I was taught, and it never even occurred to me to question it.

Then I met Lee.

When I looked up and saw Lee coming toward me on the second morning of the trade show, I was both intrigued and perturbed. Knowing in my heart that he wasn't going to just go away, I put on my best it's-only-for-three-more-days smile and resolved to make the best of it.

"How are you feeling today?" he greeted.

Dodging the question, I replied, "I've been thinking a lot about you. You kind of spooked me yesterday."

He chuckled with a knowing grin, "Yea. I get that a lot. Do you have time to talk?"

"Why not?" I thought cynically to myself as we relocated from the space of my show booth to a nearby bench. There, perched among distracted buyers and the bustle of commercial activity, I cut right to the chase, "So what was that all about yesterday?"

Lee told me a little more about who he was and where he worked, explaining that his company's booth was located on the floor below mine. "I was in my booth yesterday," he explained, "when God told me to go upstairs and find the woman who was in pain who had two dogs."

Being a good cessationist, my first inclination was to exclaim, "Seriously? God told you?" But I refrained. I decided to savor the entertainment factor here because it was apparent that he actually believed what he was saying. He explained that he had come upstairs and, starting at one end of the floor, began to visit with every female vendor, working his way toward me. When he began talking to me, he said he felt the physical sensation of pain that he had described to me. Upon my acknowledgment that I had two dogs, he said his pain sensation stopped, confirming that I was, indeed, the woman he had been sent to find.

"I'm not sure I'm buying that," I said. "But let's say, just for grins, that it's true. Why would God send you to find me?"

Very matter-of-factly he replied, "Because I have a message for you."

"You have a message for me from God?" I quipped with an incredulous tone of voice.

"Yep." He waited.

"I don't believe any this, you know," I clarified.

"I know." He waited again.

"Well, we've come this far." I said. "Let's hear it. What's the message?"

Without hesitation he said gently, "God wants you to tell him what you want."

The cynicism of my spirit immediately faded into bewilderment. In that very moment, something shifted in my spirit. With genuine curiosity I asked, "What do I want?"

"I don't know," he said. "That's between you and God."

We both waited.

"Oh!" He interrupted the silence. "I'm seeing a picture!" He closed his eyes and began to describe in specific detail, "I see pots. A group of pots down here together in the corner."

"Flower pots?" I interrupted.

"No. They're like clay pots. Old-fashion pots." He began to gesture with his hands, "They're down here in the right-hand corner where it's dark. But there's another pot off to the side by itself. Here on the left. It has a crack in it. It's broken, and there is a light shining from within the crack. It's shining onto the pots here in the dark corner."

At this point, I *knew* what he was describing, and, quite frankly, it was freaking me out more than a little.

He continued, "Yes. There's light coming out of that broken pot, but also oil. It's the oil of healing!"

"No. It's water." I corrected.

"It's oil." He said confidently.

"No. It's water."

"No. It's healing oil."

"No! It's living water!" I insisted.

He opened his eyes and with confusion on his face asked, "What are we talking about?"

Still dumb-founded, I explained. "You just described my most recent painting! It's entitled *Broken Vessel Filled with Living Water*, and I just finished it two days ago! No one has seen it, yet."

He didn't miss a beat, "You know you're that broken pot, right?"

"Yes. That's what I want people to see in my painting. The Bible says that if I believe in Jesus, he will cause rivers of living water to flow out of me. So will his joy, and it will come out of me through my cracks, my brokenness, and splash on to those around me. I want them to see Jesus in me – not just my physical limitations or my pain."

He shifted his posture, leaning in to ensure that I was listening. "You are that broken pot," he assured me, "But it's the oil of healing that will come to you and then *out of you* onto others."

We waited again.

"Pray about it," he said as he got up to leave. "I'll come back tomorrow, and we can talk some more."

BLUE TUNNEL

"God wants you to tell Him what you want." What an odd thing for Lee to say. I spent a lot of time pondering that question. What do I want?

Surprisingly, I couldn't come up with an immediate answer. I felt more inclined to count my blessings than to focus on "wants." Yes, I dealt daily with limited mobility and severe chronic pain, but I was still able to work. I could afford pain medications to keep me moving. I was single and living alone, but I had the support of family members to help and encourage me. I was blessed with Christian friends, a supportive business partner, and an attentive church family. I loved my work as an artist and entrepreneur. But most importantly, I enjoyed a personal relationship with Jesus Christ in whom I found my rest and my contentment. In light of all that, how could I focus on what I did not have?

In that moment, I determined in my heart that if I truly trusted in a loving, all-knowing God he would know what I wanted without me telling him. So, Lee's directive was a moot point for me. God would give what God wanted to give, and I trusted him to do just that. Case closed. Yet, that question echoed around in my spirit, and I couldn't shake it: What do I want?

In spite of my pain level that third morning of the trade show, I headed downtown with a sense of anticipation. I couldn't stay home today. This Lee character was intriguing, and, on some level, I found him entertaining. Would he show up again today? What odd thing would he say?

By the time I stepped into my booth and the bustle of commerce engulfed me, I had forgotten about Lee all together. The morning was passing quickly in the midst of painting and customer interactions when I looked up and saw him standing across the aisle. Thoughts of stalking crossed my mind again. I finished up with my customer and then acknowledged Lee as he approached.

"I had a dream about you last night." He stated matter-of-factly as he stepped into my booth.

"Really?" I responded with a incredulous tone and with a heightened sense of warning rising up in me.

"In my dream you were running beside a blue tunnel."

With a sense of relief I reassured myself that in spite of the evidence before me, this guy was probably more just odd than creepy. I relaxed and stated bluntly, "Running? Not me. I can't run."

He smiled that knowing grin that was beginning to annoy me. "God is going to heal you, and you will run beside a blue tunnel."

"If you say so," I said dismissively and refocused my attention back on business.

Apparently undaunted by my rudeness, he happily replied, "I'll keep praying." As he turned to walk away, he gave a wave of his hand and cheerfully added, "See you tomorrow!"

"Yeah, right. Tomorrow." I grumbled under my breath, dismissing this guy as not only odd but annoying. I consoled myself with the thought that I only had to put up with him for one more day. I gave him no further thought as I greeted the next customer and went back to work.

A productive afternoon passed, followed by the blessing of an uneventful commute home. Pulling up into my driveway, I noticed a shipping box on the front porch? "Hum." I wasn't expecting a package and thought it peculiar. I parked my car, greeted the dogs, dropped my keys on the table and went to investigate the mysterious package. The return address on the UPS label indicated that it was from a distributor of pet supplies. "That's strange," I thought and set it aside to deal with it later.

No sooner had I walked away from it when my thoughts turned to Gracie and Stella. Both are therapy dogs, and we often volunteer with a service organization. I could not recall having ordered any pet products for them, but in that moment I remembered a conversation I'd had with our group's service coordinator. She had invited me to participate in some casual park activities with the dogs. "We're all chipping in to buy agility course equipment for the dogs. Wanna join us?"

I assured her that I'd love to participate; but, because of my physical limitations, I would not be able to run my dogs through agility obstacles. "We'll do the running for you!" she happily responded. I readily accepted her invitation, and we determined the dollar amount of my donation to the equipment purchase. I left the purchasing details to her and gave it no further thought - until the package arrived.

"Well," I thought to myself, "At least the mystery's been solved."

I settled in for a quiet evening of dinner, a shower, pain medication, and some light reading. It had been a long day, and I headed to bed early. Locking doors and shutting off lights, I bumped into the package and wondered why the agility equipment would have been sent directly to me and not collected centrally. Curiosity got the better of me, and I decided to open the box.

IN JOY!

Totally unprepared for what was inside, I made my way through tape and packaging material to expose its contents. Lifting it from the box, I was stunned to discover an expandable agility tunnel. A tunnel. A blue one. I was holding a blue tunnel in my hands as Lee's words from earlier that morning came crashing in on my emotions, "In my dream you were running beside a blue tunnel."

AN UNEXPECTED ENCOUNTER

CHAPTER 2:

AT THE MERCY OF PAIN

ICY FALL

Here in Texas we get occasional ice storms during the winter months that seem to sneak in under the cover of night. They greet you the next morning with an awesome silence that hangs in the air and is broken only by the sound of tree limbs groaning and cracking under the weight of the ice. You nestle further down under the covers as you consider your response to the question you can't avoid for much longer: Should I stay home today or brave the weather conditions to get to work?

And so it was with me eighteen years before I ever pondered the impact of a blue tunnel on my life. I was thirty-one years old and focused entirely on advancing my career as a financial analyst in the banking industry. It was a world of fast-paced commercial finance in a leading national bank during a time when banks failed, merged, and restructured with unsettling regularity. No ice storm was going to interrupt the wheels of banking or my career. I pulled back the covers to face the day before me - ice and all.

Donned in running shoes and a skirted business suit, I stuffed my heeled pumps into my briefcase, hurriedly pulled on my overcoat, grabbed my keys and headed out the door determined not to be late. No sooner had I reminded myself to slow down because of the ice than I lost my footing and went pounding tail bone first down the icy porch steps. This was the moment that changed the course of my life.

AS GOOD AS IT'S GOING TO GET

"Shake it off!" I had told myself the day of my fall. I took a few days off from work to recover at home, never realizing the severity of the damage I had done to my hip and spine. A year or more passed as chronic back pain began to encroach in on a daily basis, and I developed a limp when walking. I finally sought out medical advice.

The next four years of my life were defined by doctors, medical tests, physical therapy, pain management, spinal-injury specialists, orthopedic surgeons, tears, pain, limited mobility, drugs, and lots of medical terminology. Words of explanation that fell so easily from the lips of those in the medical professions left me feeling bewildered, confused, and still in pain.

With my layman's understanding I learned that I had fractured the lower two vertebrae of my spine, and my right hip was up-slipped, rotated and wedged in the wrong position within the hip socket. Because I had not sought immediate medical attention at the time of the fall, the ill-positioned bones had begun to fuse and remodel in all the wrong positions. Spinal nerves apparently were being encroached upon by now-malformed vertebrae and were, in essence, being damaged with every movement of my spine.

With each medical opinion I heard the same prognosis: Any attempt at a surgical solution had a greater possibility of paralyzing me than relieving my pain. None of the doctors I consulted would even consider surgery as an option. I decided to consult one final doctor, my brother. I sent him my now-sizable collection of medical records for a determining opinion. There was a sobering finality in his voice on the phone that day, "Camille, I agree with your doctors. Spinal surgery is limited at best, and I don't advise it as an option for you. I'm afraid you'll have to learn to manage your pain."

Well, that was that. Medical science had spoken and so had God. I had prayed daily during this period of my life for God to show my doctors a way to give me some relief. I asked him for a breakthrough in science, effective medications, and new therapies. I got nothing from him but silence.

From a pain-management standpoint, I did everything the doctors told me to do. I lost forty pounds, tightened up muscles, practiced spine-neutral movements and spent numerous hours in pain-management therapy. At the end of four years, my doctor finally said, "This is as good as it's going to get."

I was thirty-four years old and felt like I was living in the body of an eighty-year old. I struggled to get out of bed, chairs and cars. Every movement was painful. I only had a fifteen-minute tolerance for walking, standing or sitting at any given time and spent lots of time lying down. My career was falling down around me and my world was becoming increasingly limited. I was tethered to pain medication and anti-depressants, and this was "as good as it's going to get"?

Sitting across from Lee at a Starbuck's bistro table a few weeks after having met him, he said with a touch of bewilderment in his voice, "You sound as though you don't want to be healed."

In truth, he was right. But Lee had not known me for the preceding eighteen years that I lived with "as good as it's going to get." He had no knowledge of how limited my world had become at the hands of debilitating pain. Nor did he seem to understand that pain is a thief. It's a force of evil hell-bent on robbing you of your peace and stealing your dreams of the future. It's ruthless. It's relentless. It's constant. But it's what you know, and, counterintuitively, it becomes comfortable.

It seems strange to connect the word "comfortable" with "pain," but over the years I had made my peace with pain - and with God. Although I didn't blame God for my injury, I struggled to understand why he would allow it. Had I done something to deserve this? My Bible-believing faith hung fragilely between *"All things work together for good for those who love God and are called according to His purposes"*[5] and the Lord's declaration that *"My ways are higher than your ways."*[6] My intellectual reasoning told me that although I couldn't understand God, I could still trust Him. My heart, however, felt abandoned.

But I determined in my soul that my will was stronger than my heart. I made a conscious choice to suppress my heart's disappointment. I set my mind on trusting God even if I couldn't understand how "this is as good as it's going to get" became his "good" for my life. Stoically, I carried on until I found myself a few years down the line at the precipice of another choice.

HOPE DEFERRED

Those eighteen years of chronic pain hung like a weight between "Tell God want you want" and "You act like you don't want to be healed." I could no more explain to myself, let alone Lee, how remarkably devastating it would be for me to open myself up to such a hope. My peace with God was a fragile house of intellectual logic: God is sovereign. I am not. God chooses to leave me in pain. I have no choice but to accept that. God loves me but not enough to heal my pain. Therefore, I must not be worthy enough to receive God's favor.

But I had resolved that, in spite of my unworthiness, God was still worthy. My love for Jesus outweighed my sense of divine injustice, and I determined over the years that pain would not define me. I would not be one of those people who complained all the time or constantly drew attention to their misery. I focused my faith on endurance, *"Fighting the good fight,"*[7] and determination would be my weapon of choice.

With the first movement of each day, I was awakened by pain. My morning prayer was one of daily pleading, "Lord, help me! I can't do this today without you." Bracing for the first jolt of weight-bearing pain, I began my daily limp to the shower accompanied by reminders of God's promises:

> *"The joy of the Lord is your strength."* (Nehemiah 8:10, NASB)

> *"Rejoice always, pray continually, give thanks in all circumstances." (1* Thessalonians 5:16-18, NIV)

> *"I can do all things through him (Christ) who strengthens me."* (Philippians 4:13, ESV)

In spite of the unworthiness I kept locked up inside, I sincerely trusted in God's plan for my life. Somehow, he was using my pain for his purposes. I put my faith in that. Resolved to partner with him to that end, I followed up my daily shower with caffeine, pain medication, time in God's Word, and a renewed commitment to choose steadfastness.

But what about hope?

QUESTION WITHOUT ANSWER

In the weeks following my weird but intriguing introduction to Lee, he and I entered into a business relationship over a six-week period. A local Starbuck's was our meeting place of choice. Inevitably, our business discussions gave way to spiritual ones - thought-provoking in nature, but always leaving me feeling a bit off balance. While I admired Lee's confidence and resolution of belief, his unapologetic use of the phrase "God told me . . ." tempered everything he said with warning signals going off in my head. How did God tell him things? What did it sound like? How could he know it was God and not some psychotic delusion? Better asked, was Lee himself psychotic?

In spite of my concerns, every conversation we had left me feeling more intrigued than unsettled. Lee was so sure that God was going to heal me. I wanted to join him in that confidence, but how could I? To believe such a thing would require hope, and my relationship with God was too fragile to let hope arise. Better to suppress hope than to open myself up to disappointment. After eighteen years of pain, I just couldn't handle being disappointed in God - again.

To my surprise, I actually looked forward to my Starbuck's meetings with Lee. They were entertaining in the moment and thought-provoking upon later reflection. God was really doing a number on me, but I was oblivious to it at the time. After a few weeks, Lee invited me to join him and his wife for services at their church. Boy, did I resist that idea! No way was I going to put myself in one of those odd-for-God charismatic churches! I preferred predictability in my worship.

With hindsight, I'm sure God had a belly laugh over that declaration. He wasn't about to leave me in my comfort zone as he further orchestrated events around me. Continually preoccupied with Lee's original imperative, "Tell God what you want," I prayed for direction and, quite frankly, some relief from that incessant question that was being asked of me at every turn.

Instead of inquiring where I wanted to go for lunch, my friends asked, "What do you want?" Instead of providing sales assistance, the store clerk asked, "What do you want?" Instead of recommending one entree over another, a waiter asked, "What do you want?" Those same exact words - over and over again.

"What do you want?" And then I got my answer in the newly-revealed title of an upcoming sermon series at my church: "Jesus, We Want What You Want."

Finally, there was my answer! The only thing I wanted was whatever God wanted for me. How could I go wrong there? I excitedly shared my revelation with Lee at the next opportunity and, to my bewilderment, received a serious reprimand. "Camille," Lee said gently, but sternly, "God did not send me to find you so you could give him some preacher's answer. God wants to know what *you* want. Tell him what you want."

"But I don't know!" I blurted out.

"That's OK," he reassured. "Just keep praying about it."

RUN OR EMBRACE?

All of my interactions with Lee prompted me to want to learn more about spiritual "gifts." He obviously had something that I didn't. He was confident in his faith and convinced that he was hearing directly from God. Quite frankly, my skepticism was being whittled away with every encounter with him. He knew things! Things he had no way of knowing, but he did. Remember the blue tunnel? And the yet-to-be-revealed painting? Every conversation was steeped with similar uncanny "knowings."

I hazarded to bring up the subject with my immediate circle of church friends, knowing that I would be pushed back with explanations that God only released spiritual gifts during the time of the apostles. Once they died, so did the gifts. "We have the Bible to guide us now." was the definitive dismissal.

But that wasn't enough for me. I somehow had to explain Lee - not to them, but to myself. Was God really behind Lee's "knowings" or was I being drawn toward something occult? Was I setting myself up for an even bigger disappointment in God? Or worse, some manipulative scheme of fraud? Something about Lee was drawing me in, but I was reluctant to go against what I had been taught my entire life: God just doesn't work that way in the modern world.

I sought the advice of a trusted colleague whom I knew to be the wife of a Pentecostal[8] pastor. Trusting that she could help me make sense of all this, I told her about some of my encounters with Lee and asked her for a better understanding of these "gifts." True to her gracious nature, she did not try to convince me of theological truths or denominational imperatives. She simply encouraged me to listen to my heart and trust that God would direct me.

In response to my request for specific advise on whether or not to accept Lee's invitation to attend his church she replied, "What do you want to do?"

Aargh! There was that question again! She had no foreknowledge of that question's gnawing recurrence, and, once again, I had no response to it.

"Go to his church," she advised. "It may be different than what you're used to, but think of it as an adventure. Before you go, though, be sure to ask God to give you either total peace or complete unsettling so you'll know whether this whole experience is from him or not. Then you can decide to either run from it or embrace it."

CHAPTER 3:

DIVINE SET UP

BATHED IN HONEY

Determined that it was better to get this over with than to wait, I made plans to attend Lee's church. Sounds like a simple decision but, because of my physical limitations, the logistics were daunting. I could only drive for fifteen minutes or so before losing the feeling in my right leg. Lee's church was forty-five minutes away, but there was no way I was going to invite a friend to drive me. If I was going to go to this crazy, charismatic church, I was going to do it alone.

Sunday arrived on the heels of a restless, pain-filled night, but I was determined to get this obligatory church visit behind me. Knowing that Lee would be expecting me, I gathered all the determination I could muster and began my trip across town. I drove in short increments, stopping periodically to get out and recover the feeling in my leg. It was not the most efficient way to travel, but it was working until I hit crawl-speed, detoured construction traffic. Pain and irritability intensified with every creeping mile.

Needless to say, I was not in the most worshipful mood when I arrived at Lee's church forty minutes late. Pulling into the last available handicap-parking space, I thought cynically to myself, "If this church is so great at healing, why aren't all these handicap parking spaces empty?" Then, muttering under my breath about a "wasted trip," I extracted myself from the car and tarried a moment to recover steady footing before heading inside.

The church itself was located, not in an actual church building, but in a retail shopping center. This fact alone rekindled the notion that this whole thing was probably a bad idea. I carried my skepticism, pain and irritability with me as I opened the glass door and stepped inside.

Finding the lobby empty, I consoled myself with the thought that, at the very least, I could slip in unnoticed for the last few minutes of a sermon, make my appearance to Lee, and then leave. "Piece of cake, Camille! You can do anything for fifteen minutes."

But immediately my hopes of a speedy retreat were dashed by the sound of worship music coming from behind the closed doors ahead of me. Don't get me wrong. I love worship music. But this told me that they were still in the worship portion of the service, and it was going to be a long morning.

I slipped into the back of their meeting room, allowing my eyes to focus in the darkness and take in the scene before me. The room was full of energy and excitement as people sang in response to the upbeat worship music. Hands were raised. People were swaying and singing to the music. Four little girls were dancing at the front with joyful, un-choreographed abandon. A woman was painting on a canvas to the right of the platform. Two men were standing in the aisle praying together. Several worshipers were waving poled flags in response to the music. And then, suddenly, a bolt of lightning hit the top of my head.

It wasn't an actual lightning bolt, of course; but the suddenness of the sensation was electrifying and words fail to adequately describe the experience. I felt as if thick, luxurious, warm honey was being poured on top of my head in lavish quantities. It slowly saturated my hair and began to fall to my shoulders removing with its wake every ounce of stress, tension, and consternation I had carried in with me. As the liquid continued to flow in slow progression down my arms, I tried to make sense of what was happening. Looking at my hands as this supernatural balm seemed to engulf them, I fully expected to see tangible evidence of this mysterious liquid dripping off my hands. I could not see it, but the sensation was real, nonetheless.

In the realm of physical time, this electrifying sensation traveled through my body in mere seconds; but the supernatural experience of it was slow and leisurely like the self-indulgent luxury of an amazing massage. There seemed not a measure of tension left in my entire body as I stood in its aftermath asking, "Lord, what just happened?" He answered with one gentle word that immediately popped into my mind:

Peace.

I GOT NOTHING

This peace was more than relaxed muscles and an undisturbed mind. It was an unlocking of something deep within my being, and in that moment I remembered. Facing the daunting drive to Lee's church earlier that morning, I had prayed, "Lord, give me total peace or complete unsettling." I now had my answer. Jesus had simply turned the key in my heart's lock and poured in His peace. I cannot describe it any other way than to say that it felt "holy" - weighty, pure, and reverent.

A shift of my weight and the resulting jolt of pain brought me back to reality. With worship still in progress I continued to process this whole give-me-peace experience. It crossed my mind that maybe this is what Lee means when he says, "God told me . . ." and maybe there's something to this odd-for-God way of interacting with the Divine. At this point, it was at least worth considering.

The service eventually wound its way toward a sermon, the focus of which was Jesus' Kingdom authority both here on earth and in heaven. I heard nothing radical or off-putting. They just seemed to have a heightened expectation of seeing God work supernaturally. Much to my chagrin, this became more evident at the conclusion of the service.

Being such a small congregation, it was apparent to all that I was a visitor. And, having stood at the back near the door for the entire service, I was perfectly positioned to be greeted by many on their way out. Only they didn't leave. They seemed to be waiting - for what I did not know. Quickly, a pattern of interaction began to emerge.

First, two young men thanked me for coming, saw my cane, and then asked, "Are you going up front for healing?" While waiting for my response (which would most certainly be delayed due to my dumbfounded tongue), another woman approached and, gesturing toward the platform, said, "You need to go get healed." Then a third, and before I knew it a small audience of folks stood around me - waiting. For what? Did they really think it was such an easy thing to "go get healed"? It had been eighteen years!! Who *were* these people?

Feeling like a trapped animal in a cage, I was just about ready to dismiss this intrusive huddle myself when Lee stepped in to rescue me - good thing, too, because it wouldn't have been pretty. "So much for peace," I thought as the gathering began to disperse, and I tried to regain my composure. Lee and I had completed our "glad you came" pleasantries, and I was directing my attention toward the exit when he respectfully inquired, "Before you leave, would you mind if I ask one of the pastors to pray for you?" I suppose that was why he had invited me here in the first place. I agreed readily with what I hoped was a pleasant tone of voice because inside my head I was screaming, "Just get me out of here!"

So I found myself up at the altar "getting healed." There were now four of us in this newly-formed huddle: myself, Lee, the pastor, and another woman. With my consent, the woman put her hand on the small of my back as Lee pulled out a tiny vial of oil and touched a drop to my hand. Cynically, I thought to myself, "Let's get this over with," as we all held hands and waited for the pastor to begin his prayer. After a few seconds of hesitation, he looked up at me and said, "What do you want?"

Can you believe it?!! There was that nagging questions again! I shot daggers of accusation at Lee, but his returned expression told me that he was as startled by the question as I was. "I promise," he assured me. "I never told him anything!" Turning my attention back to the pastor and his dangling, unanswered question, I stated resolutely and emphatically, "I want nothing more nor anything less than God wants for me." As my attitude hung defiant there in the air, the pastor prayed for healing.

Nothing. I got nothing. No relief from pain. No supernatural healing. Nothing. Truth be told, the only sensation I had was the feeling of heat in the hand Lee had been holding. I dismissed it, said my pleasantries, and then "got the heck out of Dodge City!"

Needless to say, God and I had a heated discussion in the car during my arduous drive home. Well, in truth, it was a one-sided rant on my part: "God, why are you putting me through this? The peace thing was cool, but it sure didn't last! Is this some cosmic game of humiliation you're playing at my expense? Well, it's working. . . I *knew* not to get my hopes up!!"

MY SECRET

Have you ever had a long-held, fully-embraced belief about yourself? No matter what evidence arose to the contrary, you still held firm to your conviction because somehow you just knew it was true? Aware of my "secret" from early childhood, I kept it hidden from my parents, siblings, teachers, and schoolmates. It did not originate with them. In fact, none of them even seemed to be aware of it. Although I never stayed consciously focused on it, my secret was always with me, and my life experiences as a young adult seemed to confirm its validity. Since I couldn't change what was true, I allowed it to become the filter through which I processed every life experience. It was what I knew to be true about myself:

I am unlovable.

I hope you'll continue reading my story so you'll know that I eventually came to understand that there is a difference between what is "true" and what is the "Truth." It is true (with a lower-case "t") that I believed the lie that I was unlovable, along with all the accompanying baggage that Satan wanted me to drag along with it - fear of rejection, fear of isolation, fear of failure, fear of discovery, and a crippling fear of the future.

But the Truth (with a capital "T") is that I am a *"new creation"*[9] in Christ. The Bible says that Jesus paid the price for all my fear and negativity when he gave up his life on the cross and rose to life again. He defeated death so I could experience his freedom. I believed that to be true but had no frame of reference for experiencing the Truth of that in my own life.

Decades of distorted Bible teaching from well-meaning but misinformed teachers had unwittingly shrouded the Truth. The Bible tells me that I am a *"new creation in Christ. The old is passed away; Behold, the new has come."*[10] Yahoo for me! - Except, I had been taught that the demarcation between old and new occurs when you die. Freedom in Christ was something to be secured here on earth but not experienced until you cross over into Heaven.

So I was stuck here on earth with a personal theology that had somehow morphed into a fully-embraced belief that, because I was unlovable at my core, I had to earn God's love. I unknowingly jumped on the band wagon of "performance" Christianity - an endless cycle of guilt-driven tasks of obligation: go to church, read your Bible, set aside quiet time with God, keep a prayer list, be kind to those around you, don't sin, don't be selfish, visit the sick, give money to the church, help the poor, and volunteer for everything!

Seems like a list of positive, morally-sound behaviors until you attach to them a motivation factor. As futile as it sounds to me now, I was trying to do everything "right" so that I could manipulate God into loving me. What followed in its wake was a lifetime of disappointment, resentment, frustration, and uncertainty. I chose to love God because I knew he was the only person who *could* love me, but I never knew where I stood on his cosmic scale of value. Only upon arrival at Heaven's gate would I learn if I had been successful. It's an exhausting and defeated way to live - especially, when you look so "Christian" on the outside.

And such was the state of my heart as I chastised myself on the way home from Lee's church, "I knew not to get my hopes up!" Yet, somehow I had let my guard down and allowed Lee's confidence to invade my defense mechanisms. I kicked my determination into overdrive and, by the time I pulled into my driveway that Sunday afternoon, I had suppressed my disappointment in God – again. With newly-fortified strongholds in place, I determined to shut down my friendship with Lee. Enough was enough.

BEST SERVED OUTSIDE

The phone rang on the following Tuesday morning, "Hey! Lee here." He proposed a business meeting to which I curtly declined with a short, decisive answer to the agenda question he wanted to discuss. He insisted. I declined a second time, "No, Lee. I'm done." True to his nature, he did not back down, "Camille. Give me an hour. One hour. Let's talk this through." We both knew we would not be discussing business. I reluctantly agreed, consoling myself with the opportunity before me, "Well, at least I can give him a piece of my mind!" And that I did.

Seated at a table with his Starbuck's fare, he stood up as I entered the room. "Can I get you anything?" he offered. Honestly, I can't remember if I accepted the offer or not. I had an agenda and nothing was going to distract me. He did not have to have the gift of "knowing" to realize that the conversation I had in mind was best served outside.

No sooner had we relocated to an outdoor bistro table, when my spew of accusation erupted, "How dare you! Who do you think you are? Who are you to think you've got God wrapped around your little finger? Stop talking about healing. It hasn't happened. It's not going to happen. And, by the way? You and all your church buddies are really bad healers!! So, stop it. Stop talking about it. Stop praying for me. Stop it! I've had enough."

He never flinched or tried to interrupt me. He allowed me to vent to my conclusion. After a brief silence he said, "Camille, we're called to pray. We leave the outcome to God." In my mind, that settled the issue. God doesn't love me enough to heal me, so that was that. At least I could shut down hope and return to normal. We waited again.

In characteristically "Lee" fashion, he broke the silence by asking a seemingly extraneous question, "So, Camille, God told me to ask you how you feel about the dream he gave you on Sunday night?"

I shot him an incredulous look meant to silence him as further anger began to rise up inside me. He continued, "God woke me up around 3:00 am and showed me the dream you were having about the white door."

That was it! I'd had enough of this. I grabbed my cane, stood up with uncharacteristic vigor, and slammed my hand down on the table in anger. Pushing my chair back against the wall I let him have it: "Eighteen years, Lee. It's been eighteen years! I don't think God wants me to be healed. It's been too long, and I don't have enough faith to believe for this!"

With my angry words hanging there exposing my defiance and frustration, Lee assured me gently, "That's OK, Camille. I have enough faith for both of us."

I had no idea what to do with myself at that point. I dropped back into my chair in a posture of exhaustion. As we sat facing, not each other, but the street scene before us, the only sounds to be heard were those of commerce and traffic.

Finally, Lee broke the silence and began to try and refocus my attention. "Listen. We don't have to talk about all that. Let's talk about your website, instead. There's plenty we need to discuss."

He took out his notebook and began talking specifics, but I didn't have ears for it. I couldn't focus on his words. I abruptly interrupted him, "OK. OK. Tell me about the dream!"

His uncanny "knowings" both intrigued me and annoyed me - especially since I was trying my best to shut down both God and Lee. How could he have known that I had had a dream Sunday night and was awakened by it around 3:00 am?

DREAM REVEALED

I listened as he described with striking detail the dream which I could recall with exact clarity. In the dream I was standing in front of a door - nothing grand, just a simple, white, residential door. It was encased with white molding within a white wall. I had no other awareness of what was around me. Was I in a hallway? An adjoining room? Outside? I had no clue other than I was standing in front of this white door.

I knocked on the door. No one answered. I reached out to turn the knob. It was locked. I began to wiggle the door knob and knock on the door simultaneously. I had no fear of danger and no one was chasing me. But an increasing urgency was rising up, and I knew that I had to get on the other side of the door. Knocking turned into pounding as I called out, desperate for someone on the other side of the door to hear me.

No answer. No one could hear me! Panic was beginning to overtake urgency when, suddenly, the hinge pin in the upper right-hand corner of the door flew out of its casing. I heard it. Swoosh! In the same moment that I ducked to avoid impact with the hinge pin, the door itself opened from the upper-right corner downward with such force that it knocked me to my knees - not the door itself, but the brilliant light that came flooding out from behind it. It engulfed me with its power, and then I woke up, my heart pounding inside my chest.

Having been taught my whole life that dreams are simply the inconsequential ramblings of the subconscious mind, I dismissed the dream in its entirety. I never gave it any further thought until that Starbuck's moment when Lee brought it back to my remembrance by describing it with exacting detail.

How could he know that?! My anger gave way to resignation as he moved from telling me about my dream to interpreting it for me. "This is crazy," I thought to myself as he continued.

"Well, let's think about this," Lee pondered aloud. "There's a door before you that you can't open. The door is locked. You have no key or other conventional means with which to open it, and no one on the other side is responding. But when the door opened, it opened with forceful power in a way you didn't expect and with consequences you didn't expect."

He let the interpretation hang there between us, expectantly waiting for revelation to hit me.

"So, Camille," he prodded gently, "What's behind the door that you want?"

With those words came revelation. It felt like my mind was a computer and God had simply downloaded new data - only it didn't quite compute. Not, yet, anyway. I knew I had the answer that had so long eluded me, but I couldn't actually articulate it. I just *knew*!

In the suddenness of the moment I turned to Lee with both excitement and enlightenment in my voice, "Lee! That's what this is all about, isn't it?! You. Me. All of this." He grinned knowingly as he allowed me to process. Somehow I knew that God was connecting the dots for me, but I didn't yet know what it meant. I just knew that God was in the middle of all *this*.

Without inquiry or further investigation, Lee gently prodded, "Tell God what you want."

"I can't." I replied almost inaudibly. I was not withholding out of unwillingness or defiance, but simply because I didn't yet actually know what I "knew."

"Pray about it. When you're ready, tell God what you want."

Needless to say, I drove home with a mind full of thoughts to process. All my experiences with Lee during the previous six weeks had left me feeling both unsettled and, despite my best efforts, now hopeful. Hope was rising again.

Three days earlier God had released supernatural peace, and I had squandered it away with irritation at Lee and the expectations of his church family. They lived in the hopeful anticipation of what amazing thing God would do next. But processed through my filter of disappointment in God, I found their expectations both irritating and, quite frankly, naive.

But God did not leave me in my disillusionment. He found me sitting at a bistro table having just chewed out the one person whom he had sent to help me. What I now refer to as my "Starbuck's revelation" became my source of hope. I didn't ask for it. I didn't expect it. I didn't even know what it was at the time.

I didn't know because I was trying to process it through intellect and reasoning. But somehow God spoke directly to my spirit - pure, undefiled, divine communication, and the message was clearly received: *It's OK to trust me with what you want.*

DIVINE SET UP

CHAPTER 4:

MIRACLE IN THE MAKING

IS HE TRUSTWORTHY?

I had spent a lifetime filtering God through my paradigm of unworthiness. Years of personal Bible study and expository sermons had left me with an intellectual knowledge of God but no real experience of him. My faith held tentatively in the balance between Bible knowledge and an endless loop of flawed reasoning.

The Bible tells me that God is love. He is slow to anger, abounding in goodness, and full of mercy. He gives saving grace to anyone who trusts in Jesus and promises never to leave me or forsake me.[11] By faith, I accept that as truth. I choose to believe it.

In stark contrast, however, my experience of God left me feeling abandoned, hopeless, and in a constant state of guilt - not guilt as a result of unrepentant sin, but guilt as a byproduct of logic gone array. It started with the mindset, albeit a flawed one, that I am unlovable. Contrast that to the Bible's promise of a God who says he loves unconditionally. Now, I have a conflict that I must resolve.

My flawed reasoning tells me that I must increase my lovability by cranking up the intensity of my "performance" Christianity output. I put on my Christianity mask and do everything right. I even try to force myself into believing that somehow I could become lovable - if I just try harder. But to no avail. All my striving still results in unanswered prayer, isolation and, ultimately, disappointment in God himself. I suppress the inevitable resentment, and then guilt sets in. What right do I have to be disappointed in the all-knowing, all-seeing God of the universe? He is justified in keeping his distance because, after all, I *am* unlovable. And the power of that lie drives me further into the endless loop of trying to earn God's love. At the same time, I add another brick to the walls of my defense mechanism in a vain attempt to avoid feeling disappointment again. It's an exhausting way to live.

But then, on a Tuesday night in the middle of March at the age of forty-nine, I found myself forced to process an experience of God unlike any I'd previously known. Earlier that afternoon God had divinely-downloaded a truth about his nature: He could be trusted. Despite decades of experiential evidence to the contrary, I now knew in my spirit that it was true. But my mind spent the entire evening trying to pull me back into logic and reason. "Trust God? Let's look at the evidence . . . You're not really going to believe him, are you?"

I awoke the following morning with the battle still raging - both the one in my head and the one in my body. My first stirrings of the day were met with a jolt of pain that experience told me would set the stage for a "bad pain" day. At the same time, a question rattled around in my head in an unceasing attempt to extract an answer: *Do you trust me? Do you trust me? Do you trust me?* . . .

I had no control over the pain, but I could put a stop to this persistent inquisition. I mustered my will to face the inevitable surge of coming pain and, grabbing the bed covers for leverage, managed to pull myself up to a sitting position. With my feet now propped up on the sideboard of the bed frame, I took a deep breath to steady myself against the now-settling wave of pain, and began to pray with uncharacteristic frankness:

"Lord, I have no idea what you're up to. I don't know for sure if this odd-for-God Lee character is really from you, but it seems like it. There was the 'blue tunnel' thing, that 'peace' thing at his church, and then the 'white door' dream he knew about. It's kind of creepy how he knows things. He's so sure! He really believes that you're going to heal me. Part of me wants to believe him, but . . . And it's weird, God, because yesterday I *felt* you. That was you, wasn't it? Can I really trust you?"

I remember waiting as those questions, spoken out loud, hung there in the air. I'm not sure if I really expected a discernible answer, but I waited nonetheless. The thoughts in my head made a last-ditch attempt to convince me of my unworthiness, but my spirit hung on to the previous day's revelation, *"It's OK to trust me with what you want."* So I continued in earnest:

"OK, God. Here's the truth. If you want to know what I really want. My true heart's desire? Here it is: I want to be pain-free."

There is was - out in the open. I had said it, and it was a monumental declaration. Up until I actually spoke those words out loud, I don't think I really knew that *that* was what I wanted. Such a statement might seem strange if you're picturing yourself in my position after eighteen years of chronic pain and limited mobility. Why wouldn't I want freedom from my suffering? It's hard to explain my hesitancy, but I knew that if God proved to be trust-worthy and Lee's confidence was realized, my world would change dramatically. Somehow, I found it easier to live in my this-is-as-good-as-it's-going-to-get reality than to face the fear of the unknown. The implications were overwhelming.

I comforted myself with a quick reminder that although I had just told God that I wanted to be free from pain; technically, I hadn't actually asked him to heal me. I didn't believe in supernatural healing, anyway. Now, it was time to do some damage control and give God some alternatives to the supernatural approach:

"So, Lord," I continued, "if you could find me a new doctor or a new drug. Maybe a new surgical alternative?"

And to further let God off the hook, or so I told myself, I added a disclaimer: "I only want to be pain-free if that's what you want for me, Lord. I want nothing more nor anything less than you want for me. I won't hold it against you if you say 'no' because you're God, and I trust you."

I waited again. Nothing. No supernatural honey-oozing peace. No divine downloads of revelation. I shifted my weight to test. Nope. No healing. So, once again, I suppressed a twinge of disappointment and steeled myself to face the slow, painful walk to the shower.

ZING! ZING! ZING!

With my shower complete, my medications consumed and my disappointment suppressed, I began my Wednesday. I went through the morning with no further thoughts of divine intervention, primarily because I had already settled the matter in my mind. Either God would heal me or he wouldn't. Period. Hope on my part would not determine either outcome. "And, besides," the thoughts in my head rationalized, "God doesn't have time for me. He's busy attending to lovable people."

My day played out like any other until shortly after lunch when I became paralyzed. Literally. I stood up from my desk chair and couldn't move forward. There seemed to be no connection between my brain and my leg functions. I sat down, regrouped and tried again. As fear and panic began to overtake me, I added anger and indignation to the mix of rising emotions, "Spit, Lord!!!! I prayed for healing and you *paralyzed* me?!!"

Trying and failing. Trying and failing. The experience lasted over an hour as disjointed and confused thoughts raced through my mind with such speed that I couldn't grab hold of even one rational thought. I didn't know what to do. Eventually, I stopped. I quit trying and simply sat to regroup my composure. "What now, Lord?"

I didn't have to wait long before I remembered that my doctors had repeatedly warned me that should I ever lose the feeling in my legs or notice any reduced leg function, I should return immediately for re-evaluation. Thankful for an actionable thought, I reached for the phone to call my doctor while wondering how I was going to "return" if I couldn't walk.

No sooner had I picked up the phone when I was knocked off-balance again by another weird, physical sensation. This time, it was worms. Not literal slimy fish bait, but more the sensation of worms. It felt like worms of electrical current were jumping around in my muscles. Zing! Zing! Zip! Zing! Traveling from my lower back around my left hip and then over to my right leg, it only lasted a few seconds. I put the phone down. Zing! Zip! It happened again. "What is going on, Lord?" The zinging and zipping continued for a few more minutes until nothing. It stopped as suddenly as it had started.

It crossed my mind in those immediate post-zinging moments that perhaps God was healing me and this is what it feels like. Hope rose. I stood up in response. With my first tentative step forward I was rewarded with movement - and then the familiar, debilitating pain that accompanied it. I grabbed my cane and took a test walk around the room. Relieved at my restored mobility, I chastised myself for allowing even a moment of hope to rise. I determined never ever to let hope arise again.

HOPE DEFERRED AGAIN

Wednesday afternoon gave way to Wednesday evening as I tried to wrap my mind around the events of the day and the whirlwind of accompanying emotions. How was I supposed to make sense of such a sequence of odd events: a promise of trust, a prayer of desire, healing denied, paralysis, fear, zinging worms, healing denied again, restored mobility, relief, pain, confusion, hope destroyed, and a reactionary vow of defiance?

Logic and reason failed me. Emotions betrayed me. God denied me. And I felt isolated and unbalanced in my desperate attempt to process not only the day's events but those of the past six weeks. I blamed Lee. I had everything under control before I met him.

I spent the remainder of the evening being tormented by my analytical mind. Mental rest would not come without a sense of order, and I simply could not make sense of any of this. Over and over. Back and forth. I tried not to think about it. Then, I tried not to think about *anything*.

Achieving no success, I redirected my blame internally. It wasn't really Lee's fault. It was mine. I knew better than to let him raise my hopes. And God? Well, I was too angry with God to talk to him about any of this. How dare he get my hopes up with his tricks to convince me that he could be trusted? And so the evening progressed in an endless loop of self-condemnation and unresolved mental conflict. To make matters worse, my chronic Restless Leg Syndrome was manifesting in full force and the intensity of my physical pain was out-pacing my emotional distress. I blamed that on the zinging worms!

"Stop it, Camille!" I reprimanded myself. Then, after determining that sleep would be the antidote to my torment, I commanded myself, "Just go to bed." I promptly obeyed but not before stopping off at the medicine cabinet for additional pain meds and a sleeping pill.

No sooner had I laid my head on the pillow than this question popped gently into my mind: *Do you trust me?* I ignored it. 11:00 pm gave way to midnight with no sleep as my mind continued to race with self-condemnation and an incessant, but soft prompting: *Do you trust me?* Midnight gave way to 1:00 am with no relief in sight as the question continued to roll around in my thoughts. I dug in my proverbial heels, refusing to acknowledge it. How could I trust God when I was so angry with him? I damned my ineffective sleeping pill. My mind raced, my legs jumped incessantly, my pain increased, and my frustration intensified. The clock flipped past 2:00 am. *Do you trust me? Do you trust me?* Always gentle, never demanding: *Do you trust Me?* The clock read 3:00 am.

Sometime around 3:30 am with the question still unanswered, I finally exhausted myself into sleep.

WHAT JUST HAPPENED?

"Someone's been here."

That was my first thought upon awakening the following morning at first light. As was my custom to delay as long as possible the pain that always came on strong with the first movement of the day, I remained still. But I had this peculiar feeling that not only had someone been there but, "Something's different." Without yet moving, I lay in bed and began to take a mental inventory of my immediate surroundings.

The bedroom door was open as it had been when I fell asleep. Because I could hear the dogs stirring on the other side of the closed hallway door, I knew they had not come in. My robe was still draped across the foot board of the bed. The closet door was slightly ajar as I had left it and, because I lived alone, I had no expectation of another person having moved anything out of place. Yet, the feeling was so strong. It felt like someone had actually been there and just left.

Have you ever had the experience of smelling someone's perfume lingering in the air long after they've left the room? It was kind of like that. Only instead of a fragrance there was a sense of weightiness - like the air in the room had been heavy but was slowly returning back to normal.

"How odd!" I thought to myself, dismissing it as the conclusion of a dream I must have interrupted with my awakening.

I braced myself for pain and rolled over to look at the clock. No sooner had I registered the time, 6:29 am, when shock set in. Disbelief rolled me back to my original position, "*What* just happened?" I lay there a moment trying to make sense of it. I tried again. This time the clock read 6:30 am, but the experience was the same.

My logic and reasoning kicked into overdrive as I tried to rationalize the impact of the shock that began to wash over me. For the past eighteen years my first movement of each day, usually to see the alarm clock, was met with excruciating pain. Today there was none.

In disbelief, I sat up. I lied down again. I stood up. I sat back down. I stood up again. After twisting to the right, then to the left, I sat back down again. "How can this be?" I tried to bring myself back into reality. "This is just your imagination, Camille. It's not real, and, if it is, it won't last. It's like a psychosomatic illness in reverse. That's it! You let Lee get into your head. Shake it off! Nothing supernatural here. It's just a temporary fluke."

Nonetheless, I walked to the shower that morning as if eighteen years of experience and fifty years of what I had always known to be true had simply vanished.

SHOCK BEFORE PRAISE

Every true follower of Jesus Christ loves to read the Gospel accounts of supernatural healings: the woman whose faith drove her to touch the hem of Jesus' robe; the man with leprosy to whom Jesus showed His willingness to heal; the paralytic man lowered into Jesus' presence by faith-filled friends, Jiarus' daughter and the centurian's servant; the blind man on the road to Jericho who cried out for mercy and received his sight; the lame man who encountered Jesus at the Pool of Bethesda and walked; the demon-possessed Gadarene delivered from the bondage of Legion; the blind man to whom Jesus restored sight by sending him to wash his mud-caked eyes in the Pool of Siloam; and so many more. Miraculous! They all had a physical need. They all met Jesus. They were all changed by their encounter with him.

We love these stories regardless of whether we believe they were limited to first-century, personal encounters with Jesus himself or whether we expect a supernatural manifestation in the modern world. We love them because they reveal the heart of Jesus, and I believe we are naturally drawn to fill in the end of these Biblical stories with something like, "And they went away rejoicing and praising God!"

Lovely as that sounds, that was not my experience. Shock and disbelief overwhelmed me as I stepped into the shower on my first pain-free day in eighteen years. It was March 19, 2009 - just a few months shy of my fiftieth birthday. On that morning everything I knew to be true about myself, everything I knew to be true about my body, everything I knew to be true about God exploded into chaos. Sometime between 3:30 am and 6:29 am that morning I gained my freedom from pain but lost my bearings entirely.

DO YOU BELIEVE IN MIRACLES?

I had no frame of reference for processing what was happening to me as I stepped out of the shower to face my pain-free world. I didn't know what to do with myself. The space around me felt so vast, as if time was somehow suspended around me. I was in shock. Like the first responses of a victim to a tragic accident or natural disaster, I was simply going through the motions in a suspended state of disbelief.

Hyper-vigilant toward every movement, my mind waited expectantly for pain. I dressed and went through my morning routine, knowing it was just a matter of time before the pain came back. This couldn't be real, could it? I passed on my pain medication that morning - not as an act of faith, but in an effort to better control the mix of uncertainty. When the pain came back I wanted to be fully aware of it so I could put this all behind me and get back to normal.

Doesn't that seem weird? Looking back now, it seems weird to me, too. But in those first hours of trying to make sense of my new reality, I *wanted* to have my pain back. I wanted "normal" back. *That* was what I knew. *That* I could handle.

As was my regular morning discipline, I tried to quiet myself before the Lord - to read my Bible and pray. But quiet could not break through my distress. How could I talk to God, now? I didn't know him at all now. The God I knew only healed like this in the stories of the Bible. This was 2009! And I was unlovable! How and why would God heal *me*? I could not fathom how to make sense of the enormity of it. Fear began to rise up when, suddenly, I was saved by the proverbial bell.

The phone rang. It was my neighbor Amanda asking for some assistance with a computer issue. Grateful for the distraction, I headed next door determined not to mention what had happened that morning. How could I explain to someone else what I could not yet explain to myself?

She greeted me cheerfully at the door and invited me in. I followed her down the familiar hallway to her office as she described her email malfunction. Although I heard every word, I processed none of them. Totally unable to focus on the task at hand, I finally blurted out, "Amanda, I *have* to tell you something."

The story of my morning gushed out of me with relief. I had no idea of what her reaction would be, but at least I had told someone. It was at least out there now. Sitting at her desk, I waited for her response as she stood in the doorway. With much-appreciated gentleness in her voice she reminded me of a peculiar conversation she and I had had a month or so earlier.

As a pilates instructor, Amanda had asked permission to show me some exercises she felt could help with my pain. Hesitantly, I agreed to her request knowing that physical exercise of any kind meant pain for me. But having agreed, I lay there on the floor mat of her studio listening attentively as she began my orientation to *Pilates 101*. Instructing me to relax so she could help position my body for the first exercise, her concentrated focus seemed suddenly interrupted as soon as she touched me. She looked at me intently and, seemingly out of the blue, she asked "Do you believe in miracles?"

At the time, it had been just another peculiar question - not unlike all the peculiar ones being asked by Lee during the same time frame. But I had not yet told her about Lee, and I never really connected their odd questions together until the morning of my healing when Amanda brought it back to my memory. I remembered having given her an open-ended but somewhat dismissive answer. "Yes. I believe miracles are possible. My God is big enough, but I have no personal experience with them."

Now, standing there in the doorway in response to my unfolding story, she said, "When I touched you that day and asked if you believed in miracles, I sensed in my spirit that you were not meant to carry that pain in your body. Let's wait and see. I believe this is your miracle."

Returning to the task at hand, I fixed her email problem and said my goodbyes. I arrived back home a few moments later and was greeted by the sound of the phone ringing as I inserted my key into the lock. After hurriedly opening the door, I ran - yes, ran - to catch the phone before the answering machine beat me to it. I pickup up the receiver, momentarily stunned by the realization that I had just run - without pain. In response to my delayed "Hello," I heard the familiar, husky voice, "Lee here."

No surprise there. Of course Lee would call on this day of all days. No small talk today. He stated quickly the purpose of his call, "Just wanted to confirm. Blue font for the titles on your home page, right?" To my simple but affirmative "Sure," he responded cheerfully, "Great! Talk to you later."

In stunned silence I thought to myself, "He knows. He has to know. He always knows." I replaced the phone on its cradle and determined, "He knows. He's just messing with me." Fully expecting him to call back with a belly laugh and a "Gotcha!" I waited. He never called back.

CHAPTER 5:

FOREVER CHANGED

A WALK TO THE PARK

So what does one do with no pain after eighteen years on an afternoon free of obligation? I decided to take my freedom for a spin. After leashing up my dogs, Gracie and Stella, we headed out for a walk (without my cane or car) on that incredibly gorgeous Thursday afternoon. The dogs seemed disoriented as I directed them down the street toward the park to which they would normally ride in the car. I was a bit disoriented myself. "How weird is this?" I thought as I tried to take in the enormity of the experience. I was *walking* to the park!

The park was empty that afternoon as both dogs waited obediently for instructions once I had removed their leases. I gave them the release command and they responded in customary fashion - Stella was born to run; Gracie to wander aimlessly. Normally restricted to wait, watch, and call Stella back if she ran out of sight, that day I walked the entire six blocks of the park's length myself - twice! Both dogs seemed to sense the uniqueness of the experience for all three of us as they heeled up toward the end without being called to do so.

Still unleashed, Stella suddenly bolted out ahead of me and then stopped on a dime and looked back as if to say, "Watch this!" She then took off running around a small group of trees. Circling back, she danced around me in what seemed like an invitation to join her. I took the bait! Together we ran around those trees as if it was a monumental orbit around the moon. For me it was. Thoroughly winded after a 30-second sprint around that silly group of trees, I collapsed in delight and rolled around the grass with my beloved dogs. "Is this real, Lord?" I cried out in my first moments of true celebration.

MY ONE DAY?

He loved to tell the story of his "one day." Forty years my senior, he was a long-time family friend who suffered from debilitating pain and limited mobility as a complication of childhood polio and degenerative spinal disease. In the later years of his life we shared a unique bond. I called him my "Pain Hero" and tried to model myself after his example. He bore his painful condition with a pastor's heart that was more intent on encouraging and uplifting others than complaining or focusing attention on his own plight. I admired him greatly.

Only in private moments, just the two of us, did he share his struggle with pain. Well into his eighties and even during my last visit with him, he always had a word of encouragement for me, swapping pain management remedies and laughing at his perspective of the Lord's sense of humor.

"I've mentored many a young pastor in my day," he'd say, "But I never dreamed I'd be a pain mentor!"

"Hero." I corrected, "Pain *hero*!"

"Yes, of course, hero." He laughed and transitioned into the story I knew he would tell - one I knew word for word, but loved to hear anyway. The telling of it flushed his face with joy as he began, "Did I ever tell you about my one day? I was a young man in my fifties . . ."

What followed was his retelling of a memory forever etched in his heart and retold time and again over the course of three-and-a-half decades. It was the story of when the Lord gave him one, pain-free day - one amazingly miraculous day - sandwiched within a lifetime of debilitating pain. He remembered that day with such fondness, telling me how he felt and what it meant to him. He never questioned why it was only for one day, never resented God for the brevity of it, nor even tried to explain it. It just was - his one day of miraculous freedom from pain. I loved how he relished it as evidence of God's faithfulness. I aspired to his level of faith, feeling woefully inadequate by comparison.

Memories of this gentle, yet mighty, man of faith flooded my heart as I walked back from the park on what I thought might turn out to be my own "one day" experience. With Gracie and Stella matching my now pain-free stride, I asked the Lord to give me the grace to receive the day as a gift. Had my beloved Pain Hero still been alive, I would have driven straight to his house and knocked on his door knowing that he would have welcomed me in with open arms and a heart of celebration.

When my head finally hit the pillow at the end of my first pain-free day in eighteen years, I felt overwhelmed by what had happened. What a day! I tried not to analyze the impact the events of the day would have on my future. I tried not to think about my future at all. I simply thanked the Lord for my "one day" experience and drifted off to sleep.

SOMETHING'S DIFFERENT

When I awoke without pain the following day I knew that my life would be forever changed and that thought brought more trepidation than joy. With the absence of physical pain came a torrential flooding of fear and anxiety. My tightly-managed, controllable life had exploded into uncertainty and my fear of the future kicked into overdrive. Even my immediate future loomed ominously before me as I considered how to tell my friends and family. What will they think? What if I tell them today and tomorrow the pain comes back? What if they don't believe me? What if they do?

Suppressing my fear and mustering my courage that Friday morning, I headed off to the office to face the uncertainty. During my short commute I decided that no big announcement was warranted. I would simply share my news in private conversations if the subject arose naturally. (In hindsight, I think God had a good chuckle over that strategy!)

I entered the office unseen. No one was around to notice that I no longer needed my cane and that my limp was completely gone. I sat down at my desk, relieved that I could delay drawing attention to myself for a bit longer, and focused instead on my work.

Within a few minutes, I was interrupted by the wife of the Pentecostal minister who had encouraged me to visit Lee's church. She greeted me warmly and began to ask questions about an accounting issue. It was a routine, work-oriented conversation until suddenly she interrupted her own train of thought. With a puzzled look on her face asked, "What's different?"

She had not seen me walk or move about. She could not have known. I feigned uncertainty.

"No," she insisted, "Something about you is different." Before I could even respond she squealed with delight and blurted out, "Oh, my God! You've been healed! You have, haven't you?"

Her exuberance took me off guard as I attempted to reel her in, "Yes. But don't tell anyone. I'm not ready . . ." No way was this going to be revealed in private conversations! She turned toward the accounting office and called out, "Come quick. Camille's been healed!"

Within minutes I was being cheered on by a small circle of excited friends, "Tell us! How did it happen?" Their commotion sparked curiosity throughout the office and, before I knew it, I found myself telling a room full of people the story of how I had met Lee and now, six weeks later, I seemed to have been supernaturally healed. It was a surreal moment for me. The cat was out of the bag, and although not everyone was ready to jump on my bandwagon with abandon, I was greatly relieved that acceptance had trumped rejection.

Having been encouraged by the reaction of my co-workers on Friday, I bravely faced on Saturday, what was for me, the daunting task of telling my immediate family - my parents that morning and my eldest brother and his wife that same evening. I assumed they would be filtering my claim of healing through the same theological lens that I was taught growing up.

Since I was still trying to come to grips with my own new reality, I greatly feared the possibility that they would respond negatively. But, much to my relief and their credit, once again grace triumphed over rejection. They each listened supportively as I relayed my story of encountering Lee and receiving my supernatural healing. Their initial response I would characterize as accepting but guarded. I knew in my heart that they, too, would need more time to process the reality of it. After all, I was still trying to make sense of it myself.

Finally, I placed a phone call to my brother who lives in Florida who is both a practicing medical doctor and the pastor of his church. Based on my knowledge of his life's experience, I knew he would be predisposed to celebrate my news. He listened with great interest and upon its conclusion responded with calm but underlying excitement in his voice, "That's way cool!"

As Saturday evening came to a close my thoughts turned back to Lee. I had not heard from him since our brief, work-related phone conversation on the morning of my healing. I couldn't conceive that he didn't "know," but his silence made me curious. I determined to go back to his church on Sunday.

TIME TO TESTIFY

"What a difference a week makes!" I thought as I drove toward Lee's church on the Sunday that followed my healing. Just a week before I had driven the same route with a sense of trepidation in my heart. In stark contrast, today my heart was filled with excitement and anticipation. I pulled into the church parking lot and parked my car. Walking through the lot, I passed an open handicap-parking space. Joy rose up at the thought of my contribution to its availability. With a smile, I entered the building in search of Lee.

I quickly spotted him, but because his back was toward me, he did not see my initial approach. He was facing a small group of men who seemed engrossed in the story he was telling about having a "God" encounter with a lady in a Lowe's hardware store. ("Good for her!" I thought.)

Standing just outside his peripheral vision, I waited so as not to interrupt his story. But although he was not aware of my presence, his audience was. Someone eventually gestured to direct Lee's attention toward me.

"You came back?" he blurted out with a startled look on his face. That made me laugh, because just earlier that week I had accused him and his church buddies of being bad healers. No doubt, I was the last person he expected to see again here at his church.

"I had to come back," I told him. "I have something I need to give you."

His expression changed quickly from initial curiosity to total confusion as I pulled out his gift from my Bible. Having cut my handicap-parking placard in half, I now extended my hand to gift it to him. What followed was absolutely delightful to me as he accepted it and began to process its significance. Excitement began to visibly rise up in him as he exclaimed, "What are you telling me?!" He moved around me hurriedly as he sought to find my cane. "*What* are you telling me?"

Gesturing toward my handicap-parking placard and, enjoying his excited confusion, I responded, "Some kind of word-of-knowledge-prophet you are! Don't you know? I don't need that anymore!"

"Oh, my God! She's been healed!" he exclaimed and turned to his buddies, "She's been healed!!" He looked back at me seeking further confirmation, "For real?!"

I laughed and confirmed, "For real." We rewarded each other with tears and a big bear hug as the excitement in the small group around us began to spread throughout the room. Within what seemed like an instant, I found myself *testifying* at the front of the room with a microphone in my hand. Who would have thought? Not me, for sure. But the genuine and spontaneous celebration of this room full of Jesus followers was electrifying, and I felt a sense of belonging.

That particular day will always be marked in my memory as "Celebration Sunday" and forever held in my heart as a sweet remembrance.

THE AFTERMATH

And so the next chapter of my life began to unfold as I tried to make sense of my supernatural encounter with a God who, until my healing, I had only yet to experience in my limited realm of the natural. I'd like to report that my undeniable physical healing catapulted me to a level of faith equal or greater to that of Lee's, but as that summer unfolded I found myself in the grip of overwhelming depression, isolation and, oddly-enough, guilt.

In hindsight, I can look back on the events of that summer with a fondness for the work of emotional healing the Lord was doing in my life. But living out that season of darkness was tormenting.

Although rejection was not the response of most to whom I told my story during the first week after my healing, it was rampant among the members of my own church family. I never dreamt that my conservative, Bible-believing friends, many of whom I'd known over twenty years, would react with such vehement negativity and, to my surprise, verbal condemnation:

"God doesn't heal that way in the world today. The Bible says so."

"What you're saying isn't Biblical; therefore, it's a lie of Satan himself."

"You've been led astray by a cult."

"How can you tell such a story? It's destructive to all of us."

"You mustn't say such things. What will people think of you?"

"Why are you trying to manipulate me?"

"This can't be true. You've been lying to us all along about being in pain."

"Hey, Camille, is it true that you were healed while sitting in rush-hour traffic on Central Expressway?"

Each and every one of these encounters took me by surprise as they unfolded. To some extent I understood their caution and confusion. My testimony of supernatural healing was as foreign to them as my first encounters with Lee and his "knowings" had been to me. To accept my story at face value would require a total shift in their theological paradigms. It would take time, I rationalized. But with each passing week, I felt more and more isolated.

Now, not only was I unlovable, but I was a freak. Why weren't my friends celebrating my healing like Lee's church had? Those people didn't even know me. And if my friends couldn't celebrate, couldn't they at least explore the possibility of my claim before condemning it?

After about a month, I made an appointment with one of the pastors of my church. Surely, he would celebrate my news and give me guidance in how to deal with the reactions from fellow church members. I remember how optimistic I felt that afternoon as I drove to his office. Finally, someone with whom I could talk, someone who would understand. He was always talking about "passionately pursuing Jesus Christ," and I had no doubt that he would celebrate with me my real-life encounter with that same Jesus.

He greeted me warmly and listened intently as I began to share my story of encountering Lee. As the story unfolded, I began to feel a shift in his demeanor. He allowed me to complete my story before responding with a theological disclaimer and a question - a question that devastated me to the core.

"This is not what we teach here, but if what you say is true, why would God heal *you*?"

With this one question, delivered with an incredulous tone of voice, he had revealed his heart's response, and sent me further down the path of self-doubt. The story I told myself in that moment was that he not only didn't believe me, but he was questioning my worthiness to be healed. I struggled with that question for months thereafter as it taunted me with haunting regularity. "Why me, God? Why would you heal such an unlovable person as me?"

I listened to this pastor continue his counsel as he gave advice on how I should respond if people asked me about my "healing." It was more a diatribe on damage control than Godly counsel. He eventually ushered me to the door with these parting words that I will never forget: "Try not to be disappointed in God when the pain comes back."

Never in my life have I felt more defeated than in that moment as I walked out of his office and made my way through the church corridor. He had opened wider the door of doubt and condemnation, and I unwittingly walked right through it. I trusted this man who had been my pastor and teacher for nearly twenty years. If he agrees with everyone else, then there must be some truth in it, right?

He must be right about one thing, I conceded: I am unworthy. And given that reality, why would God heal me? I began to feel guilty that God had healed me - and then I felt guilty for feeling guilty. Depression began to swallow me up as I agreed in my spirit with his assessment and allowed guilt, anger, and frustration to take hold.

CHAPTER 6:

FROM WHITE SPACE TO WORSHIP

JUST WHAT I NEEDED

I made the phone call in mid-June with a genuine plea for help, "Can you find me someone with whom I can talk? I need help from someone who can understand what is happening to me."

In spite of the increase in my anti-depression medication and attempts at self-assessment, I found myself floundering in a sea of isolation, guilt, and confusion. I felt as if heaven was closed to me. God had healed me and then abandoned me. My prayers felt impotent and my despair shockingly debilitating.

My brother assured me over the phone that he would find someone who could help me. "I'll pick you up at the airport."

I had no expectations as I boarded the plane to Florida, other than I trusted my brother to help me find a way to move forward. My heart was aching for unconditional acceptance as the plane touched down that July morning. Seeing him from across the airport lobby, I rushed toward him without encumbrance from a cane or pain, and landed into a bear hug of assurance.

Immediately I began to grill him, "Did you find someone? Have they been supernaturally healed, too? Do they know about supernatural healing? Is it a doctor? A pastor? One of your patients? Someone from your church?"

He was introduced to me as Pastor David, and I spent a few hours with him the following day. Experienced with decades of pastoral counseling, he was just what I needed. I retold my story of encountering Lee, receiving healing, and my subsequent struggles with depression, isolation and rejection. He listened with interest and affirmed my experience without judgment or condemnation.

He revealed that although he did not have tangible, personal experience with supernatural healings, he fully believed in their modern-day manifestations. He began to help me refocus with this simple statement: "You're in the white space between chapters."

He began to elaborate by explaining that God is writing out my story in chapters - as he does with all of us. When he brings one chapter to a close, he allows "white space" before beginning the next chapter. He continued:

"Think of the pages of any book. There is a title page, followed by a foreword or acknowledgment page, and then you turn your attention to the first chapter. There is usually white space in the header, then the chapter's title, and then white space before the first paragraph begins. At the end of the chapter there is usually more white space - sometimes half a page or more - before the next chapter begins.

"Camille, you're in the white space. God has closed a chapter in your life, and you are waiting in the white space before the next chapter unfolds. You must wait for him to begin your next chapter."

IN JOY!

Being an avid reader myself I loved this analogy, but it wasn't enough, "What do I do while I wait?"

His answer was surprisingly powerful in its simplicity: "Abide."

LEARNING TO ABIDE

I spent a lot of time that summer studying the 15th chapter of John:

"Abide in me, and I in you. As the branch cannot bear fruit by itself, unless it abides in the vine, neither can you, unless you abide in me. I am the vine; you are the branches. Whoever abides in me and I in him, he it is that bears much fruit, for apart from me you can do nothing." (John 15: 4-5,7 ESV)

"No longer do I call you servants, for the servant does not know what his master is doing, but I have called you friends, for all that I have heard from my Father I have made known to you." (John 15:15, ESV)

"If the world hates you, know that it hated me before it hated you. If you were of this world, the world would love you as its own; but because you are not of the world, but I chose you out of the world, therefore the world hates you." (John 15:18-19, ESV)

Unsure of exactly what abiding looked like in a practical way, I felt strongly that this chapter of Scripture was a minefield full of truth for me. It spoke to how I felt and what I longed to understand. The focus of my prayer life shifted from the habitual "Your will be done" to "Help me understand your will."

I began to prayerfully pose my questions to the Lord – those at the heart of my depression: Why was my healing such a derisive issue among my church family? Why do I feel so guilty? Lord, why did you choose me? What's the real truth behind this supernatural experience? Do you really speak through people like Lee? Was it real? Have you healed anyone else this way? What do I do now?

All my questions seemed to float upward and disappear into thin air without answers. I could not shake a persistent nagging to *do something*! but was at a loss as to *what* to do. Weeks went by until I awoke one morning with this thought rolling around in my head: *Paint what you see.*

At first this phrase seemed to be stating the obvious. I'm a professional watercolor artist, and I always paint what I see. But this phrase seemed so familiar as I rolled it around in my head all morning. Eventually, it came to me.

Remember my recollections of "Celebration Sunday" at Lee's church on the Sunday following my healing? During worship that morning that same phrase had popped into my head: *Paint what you see.* It was a seemingly random thought at the time because what I was seeing in that moment were people - people who were worshiping. People. That meant portraits. Having no experience with portraiture, I dismissed the thought easily and completely at the time.

Now, four months later, God was somehow connecting the dots, and I was choosing to respond in faith rather than with understanding. I made a choice to move through my depression by focusing my energy on painting a series of portraits I would later entitle, "The Heart of Worship." Photos I had taken at Lee's church were the inspiration for the series of sixteen paintings - images of Jesus-followers with their hands raised in worship, or heads bowed in reverence, or singing joyfully.

As it turned out, becoming engrossed in those paintings was my way of "abiding." I spent several months in their creation as I prayed over each one and sought further answers from God: What do these people have that I don't? Is there a truth about you, Lord, that I've missed? How can I feel the same way about you that these people do? Do you talk to all of them like you talk to Lee? How can they worship like this with such freedom? How can I have what they have?

What a paradox of thought! At the same time I was desiring to explore God in a more expressive way, the thoughts in my head rose up with familiar condemnation: "Who do you think you are? God doesn't have any truth to reveal to you. These people you're painting are freaks - emotional misfits. They don't know God any better than you. They just want attention. Emotionalism is weakness. They're weak. You're weak. Your healing wasn't supernatural. It was just a fluke. If you keep talking about it to people you'll never be accepted."

It was exhausting. But in spite of the internal conflict, I felt that somehow God was trying to call me out of the mental ruckus with a gentle, yet now familiar, prodding: *Do you trust me?*

During that summer of abiding, God orchestrated experiences and personal encounters that began to answer my questions and lead me further on my path toward discovering the spiritual nature of God.

CAN YOU BELIEVE THAT?

Shortly after my return from Florida, I attended a one-day seminar on a topic I had no interest in: Training your Theatrical Voice. I was not an actor or a public speaker, but for weeks I felt drawn to attend this event. I had no idea why, but I couldn't shake the feeling that I was supposed to be there.

It turned out to be a small gathering of about twenty people, most of whom I had never met. And the mystery of why I was drawn to attend did not reveal itself until we all went to lunch at a local restaurant. Between ordering and being served, one of the attendees demonstrated his theatrical voice by entreating across the table, "Camille, tell us your healing story." Nineteen sets of eyes awaited my response. I had no idea of the theological orientation behind those faces as I began my story, but throughout its telling my attention was drawn toward one particular young woman. Twenty years my junior, she maintained eye contact with me throughout and responded often with, "I believe you."

It was not until the end of the day's events that I was able to speak with her privately. "Why were you so insistent on my knowing that you believed my story?" I asked.

"Because of all the people who didn't believe *me*."

As she began to tell me her personal healing story, I knew that God had arranged this encounter just for me. I listened intently as she unfolded a story of being eight-months pregnant and trapped in her car under the weight of an eighteen-wheeler. There in the middle of the highway, pinned up against the steering wheel and unable to move, she prayed for the protection of her unborn daughter as first responders worked to extract her from the wreckage.

"I knew it was bad," she told me, "Blood was all over my face. I couldn't move, and I kept drifting in and out of consciousness. All I knew to do was pray and sing worship songs in my head."

In spite of her broken hip, the loss of an eye lid and lacerations on her face that would later require hundreds of stitches in her face, her unborn child was unharmed. She recalled the second day of her hospital stay as the plastic surgeon gave her the news that if they could repair the damage to her face it could take up to ten years of reconstructive surgery. "Don't get your hopes up," he admonished before leaving her room. In the silence that echoed in his wake, she worshiped.

I was awed by the strength of this young woman as she explained further, "Camille, the Lord answered my prayer. He protected my daughter and kept me alive. I was so thankful that it didn't seem to matter what I looked like."

She then began to tell the most riveting part of her story. "On the third day after the accident, I went into the bathroom," she began. Feeling the need to be alone and in spite of the protests of family and nurses, she gathered herself up out of the bed with IV pole in tow and went into the bathroom, locking the door behind her. Her first look in the hospital mirror at the damage to her face was overwhelming she recalled. "Tears wouldn't come," she explained. "I simply sat on the toilet and began to sing. It was all I knew to do."

Her song of thanksgiving came out weak and unsure. But with every note her voice became more confident. "And then this weird thing happened," she prefaced. "I felt as if I was being covered in honey and light. I know it sounds weird, but I've never felt such peace." (I nodded my understanding.)

"Overwhelmed with the Lord's presence and still singing, I stood up and raised my hands to worship. It was amazing! I was alone in a hospital bathroom, but I felt like I was in heaven. And then I opened my eyes." She described the experience of seeing her face in the mirror before her. There was no swelling, no stitched-up lacerations, and her missing eye lid had been reformed. "I looked perfectly normal." She explained.

Now, we were getting to the good part of the story! "Then what did you do?" I asked with great anticipation.

"I don't know exactly. I was in shock, I think." She recalled pulling out the IV, rushing out of the bathroom, and announcing to her attending nurses and awaiting family, "God healed me!! I want to go home now."

She described the chaos in the room as the nurses began to scramble in response. "Of course, they wouldn't let me leave," she chuckled as she recalled her experience of getting dressed and sitting in the visitor's chair of her hospital room as they paraded in one doctor after another.

"Can you believe it?" she asked me, "They didn't believe me. How could they not believe me? I was in the bathroom for fifteen minutes tops!" She recalled that they kept her in the hospital for two more days as they re-ran all their tests and were forced to admit that she had been healed.

She was released from the hospital and delivered her healthy baby one month later. "We just celebrated her tenth birthday!"

As amazing as this story was, I wanted to know how she dealt with the aftermath. "What did you do after that? Do you know why God healed you? How did your family react? What about your church? Did they believe you?" I pommeled her with a barrage of questions.

"Honestly, Camille, I was shocked at how people reacted. The hospital had taken photos of me when I was brought into the emergency room. The plastic surgeon had photos taken after the initial sutures were in place. And, of course, my family took pictures on the day they released me from the hospital. In spite of the pictures, people still didn't believe me! In fact, one of the doctors asked me if I had a twin sister. He thought we had switched places! Can you believe that?" She laughed.

In response to my further questioning, she encouraged me, "God healed me because he chose to heal me. It's as simple as that. The only thing I owe him in response is my worship. I let him handle the disbelief in others."

As I walked to the parking lot at the end of that remarkable encounter, I thanked the Lord for arranging what I knew to be a divine appointment. I *needed* to hear the story of this faith-filled young woman. I *needed* her encouragement. Because of this experience my new course of action took on a further dimension: Worship.

Abide *and* worship.

'TIL I REST IN PEACE

I had no clue how to worship. My experiences of worship in youth and young adulthood involved congregational singing with predictable uniformity - always the first, second, and last verse of any two hymns at a snail's-pace tempo during Sunday services at my church. Without disparaging the hymns that so many faithful believers hold dear, to me their lyrics were tortuous in content:

"When our days of toil shall cease, waiting still for sweet release."[12]

"I'll bear the toil, endure the pain, supported by Thy word."[13]

"When with the ransomed in glory, His face I at last shall see, 'twill be my joy . . ."[14]

"I know my mansion He prepareth, . . .and He at last will come for me."[15]

"Then He'll call me some day to my home far away, Where his glory forever I'll share."[16]

"When this poor lisping stammering tongue lies silent in the grave, then in a nobler, sweeter song I'll sing . . ."[17]

"There are heights of joy that I may not reach 'til I rest in peace with Thee."[18]

Lyrics that were undoubtedly penned to inspire faith, spoke to me a disappointing truth: My life must be endured in toil and strife until death releases me to experience the presence of God and the benefits of my saving faith in Jesus. And because my life was so dominated by undercurrents of fear, especially the fear of death, these songs set the stage for decades of distorted theology.

In reality, my "worship" had been reduced to declarations of my willingness to endure while waiting in fear. Perhaps *this* helps to explain my steadfastness during eighteen years of debilitating, chronic pain. I was "*bearing my cross*"[19] with faithfulness unto death. On many occasions with my fears disguised by surface joy, I spoke with hope deferred: "One day I'll be dancing pain-free with Jesus!" And I meant it. I looked forward to it.

And now, as this newest chapter of my life began, I was being called to abide and worship. Honestly? That seemed to me a dreary prospect - until I met Joe and Kim.

FIRST, THERE WAS AMY

But before Joe and Kim, came Amy. I adore Amy. She is a woman of strong moral character whose love for Jesus compels her to care for and reach out to others - to remind them of who they are in Christ and call out the best in them. Amy does that for me.

Several years before my healing experience, she and I had befriended each other while serving on the leadership team of a faith-based community of artists. Her spontaneity and creative spirit drew me to her, as did her youthful enthusiasm. Being around her always lifts my spirits. I love that she did not reject my healing testimony nor did she shy away from my post-healing depression.

"Just come. Everyone's invited." She assured me. "People come from all different churches. It's all about worship. You'll love Joe and Kim!"

In response to her repeated invitations, I repeatedly declined to accept them. Although I did not know Joe and Kim, I knew that they attended my church. The last thing I intended to do was open myself up to further rejection from anyone at my church.

Furthermore, my envisioning of a group of "worshiping" people sitting around singing about delayed gratification had no appeal whatsoever.

"No thanks," I told Amy again as I added another brick to my wall of defensiveness.

And then God sent me Rosemary.

THEN, THERE WAS ROSEMARY

What seemed at the time to be a chance encounter turned out to be another divine appointment. Serving as volunteers, Rosemary and I met while hanging an art show for public display. Casual, break-time conversation quickly revealed that she, too, was a member of my church and she, too, extended to me an invitation.

"Come join us for prayer." She quipped cheerfully. "We meet on Sunday mornings in the small room behind the Worship Center. There are only a handful of us, but we want what you want."

"To not be rejected?" I thought cynically to myself before responding more appropriately, "And what do we all want?"

"To experience the Holy Spirit, and invite Him to change our church culture."

"At our church?" I responded with surprise (and shock) in my voice.

LAST BUT NOT LEAST

I had no idea what awaited me as curiosity outweighed my uncertainty and I opened the door to the small room behind the worship center. A quick glance around the room revealed two glaring observations: It *was* a small room, and Rosemary was not there.

As I timidly stepped across the threshold, my hesitancy was greeted warmly by a man who stood upon my arrival and introduced himself. "Welcome! I'm Joe. I'd like you to meet my wife, Kim."

(Amy was not going to believe this!)

UNCOMFORTABLE, YET INTRIGUED

You have to love God's sense of humor! I had stubbornly refused to meet Joe and Kim at Amy's invitation, but I could not refuse God's invitation. I knew in my spirit that since God had arranged for me to meet them, they must be the people who would teach me how to worship.

I began to attend their Sunday morning prayer group. Even after hearing my healing story, they accepted me. I couldn't understand why. It felt like an oasis among all the rejection I'd experienced. The small room behind the worship center became a place of acceptance.

And I loved to hear them pray. This small band of pray-ers prayed with passion, authority and eloquence of words. I prayed with awkward word flow and weak expectations. They believed that God could and *would* change the culture at our church, and they waited joyfully for it to come about. I, on the other hand, was secretly cynical at the thought. My post-healing interactions with the leadership were evidence to the contrary. And, yet, they prayed on in faith.

Shortly after meeting them, Kim extended the same invitation Amy had: "Everyone's welcome! We meet in our home for worship on the first Saturday of every month. I'd love for you to join us."

I thought Amy was going to faint from surprise when I walked in the front door of Joe and Kim's house the following Saturday night. She was as surprised to see me there as I was to be there. As she greeted me and introduced me around, my fear-flight response became harder to suppress and thoughts in my head violently warned me not to trust these people. Fear began to rise up as the group began to settle into the living room - some on the sofas, some on the floor, others on the staircase balcony that overlooked the sunken living room. There must have been forty or fifty people there.

As Joe introduced himself and welcomed us warmly, my anxiety escalated. He laid out the format for the evening, "We'll listen to some music as we worship, then I'll share what the Lord has given me this week, and we'll have a time to minister to each other at the end."

Ministry time at the end? I didn't know exactly what that meant, but I was sure it would require "sharing" something personal with total strangers. Fear of rejection began to rise up in me as everything in my being was screaming "Bolt! Get out of here!" With a gesture of support and reassurance, Amy interlocked her arm with mine, and I chose to honor her by staying.

I confess that I was completely uncomfortable in this environment. It was free-flowing and spontaneous as Joe dimmed the room lights and played a series of contemporary Christian songs from a sophisticated sound system. The lyrics were uplifting, without a hint of suffer-'til-you-die theology, but the volume was so loud that it caused anger to rise up in me. I could not explain it at the time, but I actually got angry at Joe for playing the music so loudly.

It didn't seem to bother anyone else. A glance around the room reminded me of Lee's church as people worshiped with hands raised or kneeling on the floor. Some people sang, some sat silently. A woman was dancing around in the dark at the back of the room. It was uncomfortable to me, and yet, I was intrigued by their freedom of expression. I wondered to myself, "What are they thinking about while they worship?"

After about forty minutes of enduring the loud music, I was grateful when Joe shifted into the teaching segment. He began to talk about worship - what it was and why we do it. My interest peaked. After all, this was why I was here, right? - to learn how to worship.

My hopes of a quick fix were dashed as Joe began to explain that it wasn't something we do. It's something we become. We become worshipers when we enter into the "Presence of God." He further explained through Scripture:

"The Lord's presence inhabits the praises of his people."[20]

… IN JOY!

> *"We enter His gates with praise and thanksgiving."*[21]
>
> *"Where the Spirit of the Lord is, there is freedom."*[22]
>
> *"In His presence is fullness of joy."*[23]

This was a radical presentation of the meaning of these Scriptures. I had been taught their significance through the lens of "endure 'til you die, and then you'll experience the Lord's presence." But Joe was unabashedly telling me that I could experience it now through worship. He had set the hook, and I took the bait with cautious intrigue! Maybe this was the missing piece to explain what the people in my portraits had that I did not.

As it turned out, the "ministering to each other" portion of the evening was not as daunting as I had imagined. No one demanded that I publicly expose my fears or confess any sins. We simply broke into small groups to pray for each other "as the Spirit speaks to you" (which seemed a bit weird to me - but so had this entire evening and, come to think of it, so had the past nine months!) Amy was in my prayer group, and by the end of the evening, I left feeling strangely encouraged and optimistic about what God was up to. I also had lots to think about.

UNLOCKING A MYSTERY

In spite of my cynicism, my resistance to trust, and the annoyingly loud music, I kept going back to Joe and Kim's each month. I was initially drawn more to their welcoming acceptance than to the worship experience. But with each passing month, I lessened my defenses and trust began to seep in. So did worship.

What I began to discover about myself is that I was religious. I've loved Jesus my entire life, but my whole experience of him had been filtered through a system of "doings." I went to church services, classes, and prayer meetings. I prayed and read my Bible daily. I suffered stoically through years of chronic, debilitating pain. I practiced the moral code of the Bible and tried to avoid the "sin" activities with determined intentionality. And I trusted that someday ("in my home far away"[24]) I would be rewarded. Religion had become obligatory duties.

Over the following months something began to shift in my spirit as Joe, Kim and others in the group began to share their experiences during worship. I began to realize that I had spent a lifetime allowing fear and obligation to be my religious motivation: If I could "do" everything right, then maybe I could please God into loving me in spite of my unlovableness.

But I was situated now among a group of people who were motivated by love. They loved God and truly seemed to *know* that they were loved by him. It was central to how they worshiped. Joe continually reinforced our identity as "sons and daughters of the Most High God," reminding us that we are entitled to all the privileges offered by our position in Christ.

According to Scripture:

> *"For all who are led by the Spirit of God are sons of God. For you did not receive the spirit of slavery to fall back into fear, but you have received the Spirit of adoption as sons, by whom we cry, 'Abba! Father!' The Spirit himself bears witness with our spirit that we are children of God."* (Romans 8: 14-17, ESV)

The key to this promise seemed to pivot on being "led by the Spirit." Somehow I knew that *this* would be the key to unlock the mystery. *This* was what the people in my portraits had that I did not. *This* was what allowed Joe and Kim to worship with such freedom. *This* is what emanated from Lee. *This* was what I wanted.

CHAPTER 7:

FINDING FREEDOM

CLEANSING THE TEMPLE

May I take a momentary break in my story to remind you of a Bible story we all know? It's vital in helping me explain the next step in my journey as freedom joined abiding and worship. Here's the story from Matthew's gospel:

> *"And Jesus entered the temple and drove out all who sold and bought in the temple, and he overturned the tables of the money-changers and the seats of those who sold pigeons. He said to them, "It is written, 'My house shall be called a house of prayer,' but you make it a den of robbers."* (Matthew 21:12-13, ESV)

I always wondered why Jesus would get so angry at the merchants there in the outer courts of the temple. The religious law required the people to offer animal sacrifices, and the merchants were simply selling what the law required and providing money-changing services for weary travelers. So why all the fuss from Jesus? Couldn't he have voiced his opinion with gentle firmness and petitioned the priests to have their commerce moved to an outside location? Why the violent anger? John's version of this gospel story says, *"And making a whip of cords, he (Jesus) drove them all out of the temple, with the sheep and oxen."*[25]

Herod's temple in Jerusalem was the setting for this dramatic episode of Jesus' wrath. The structure of the temple mirrored that of Moses' temple from the earliest days of the Jewish people in that it consisted of three distinct areas: The Holy of Holies, the Holy Place and the Outer Court.

The Holy of Holies was located within the inner-most protected area of the temple. Partitioned by the sacred veil, it contained the holiest of all religious artifacts - the Ark of the Covenant. The Bible tells us that the Presence of God filled the temple and rested upon the Ark's Mercy Seat.[26] This was where God lived. So sacred was this room that it could only be entered into by the highest-ranking priest, and then only once a year after extensive, ritual cleansing to remove any hint of sin's contamination. The Holy of Holies was to be protected and respected at all cost.

The Holy Place of the temple was an enclosed vestibule located on the outer side of the sacred veil. It served as a functional area for the priestly activities prescribed by the Law of Moses. Other sacred artifacts were housed in this room: the golden altar of incense, the golden lampstand and the table of Presence. It, too, was a place of restricted access.

The Outer Court surrounded these sacred inner rooms and was open to everyone, Jew and non-Jew alike. Central to the activities of the Outer Court was the brazen altar and laver, used by the priests to offer the animal sacrifices brought by the people to fulfill the dictates of the Jewish law. This, too, should have been a place of spiritual reflection and thanksgiving but, because it was open to all people, it had been taken over by the chaos of merchandising - unscrupulous commerce, at that. In addition, the priests had neglected their obligation to protect both the sacredness of the house and the worshiper's right to worship in a place of peace. And Jesus was angry about it!

In a justified act of righteous anger and indignation, Jesus stepped into the situation with His God-given authority and shut it all down. He canceled their permission to set up shop within the temple and demanded, under the threat of flogging, that they leave. The tables were being overturned, coins were clanking on the floor, the animals were scurrying about, people were yelling, Jesus' whip was cracking, and the merchants, no doubt, were scrambling to comply. Jesus wanted them out *now*!

I wanted to remind you of the story of Jesus cleansing the temple because of Sandi.

SANDI AND HER PIGS

Quite frankly, the email I received from Sandi that afternoon concerned me deeply. "Please pray for me, now!" Came her words penned in an email from a hotel in Russia while on a mission trip. "They tried to choke me!" she reported as she hid in her hotel bathroom in order to escape the demons in the adjoining room. "Pray *now*!"

I prayed, alright. But I prayed for her sanity. I did not know her very well at that time, but demons? Really?

Sandi and I met for dinner several months after her return from Russia. Her story was riveting as she talked about seeing demons, being choked by them, people getting sick, and others in the group reporting similar phenomenon. It was fascinating to listen to this tale of adventure, but seriously?

I was about to re-direct her to a more rational line of thought when she blurted out, "I brought them back with me!"

In spite of my jaw-dropping reaction, she continued to describe the "heaviness" she had felt even after her return from Russia. "It was like I was walking around with a deep depression, but it had a 'creep' factor." She explained, "It felt creepy, and my thoughts were full of curse words. I didn't understand it. It was like that demon from the hotel room had attached itself to me, and I just couldn't shake it."

"Sandi," I interrupted vehemently, "Christians can't be demon-possessed! We're God's temple and his Spirit lives in us.[27] Demons can't live in the same place with the Spirit of God. It's impossible."

"That's what I thought, too. But I found this book." She pulled a soft-bound book from her handbag and set it on the table in front of me. "You're right about the temple. But it's different than you think."

I looked at the book's title, *When Pigs Move In* by Don Dickerman.

"He explains it in there." she said as she continued, "We have three parts just like the Jewish temple. We have a *spirit* that has a *soul* (our mind, will, and emotions) that lives in a *body*. Jesus paid the price for all sin when he died on the cross, and when we believe that by faith, the Spirit of God comes to live in our spirit, right?"

"Yes," I accented, wondering where she was going with this.

"OK. If we are the temple of God, then his Spirit comes to live in our spirit - like the Holy of Holies in the Jewish temple. But we can sin with our minds and our bodies even after we're saved, right? That's the same as the Holy Place and the Outer Court. The demons can get in there if we let them - into our mind and body."

"I don't know, Sandi, that seems . . . "

She interrupted with insistence. "I know it's true!"

"How?"

Pointing to the book she said, "I went to see this guy, and he was able to cast them out."

"Cast out what?"

"The demons." She said matter-of-factly.

"Exorcism? Sandi, are you serious?"

"They call it 'deliverance.' but it's the same thing - only without the Hollywood hype. No priests, crucifixes, or holy water. No spinning heads or spewing vomit." She clarified, "It was more like a counseling session, and now the demons are gone."

I sat there is silence. I had nothing to say.

After a few moments, she broke the silence with gentle prompting, "Jesus stepped in and cleared the temple when it was defiled, didn't he?"

AVOIDING MY OWN PIGS

Needless to say, I had a lot of questions for God as I left Sandi and drove home that evening. No answers. Just lots of questions. I unlocked the back door, dropped my keys on the counter, along with Sandi's book, and determined to just let Sandi be Sandi. "That's her gig," I thought dismissively. "Christian's can't have demons."

IN JOY!

Several weeks went by as I walked around that book on the counter. I never moved it. I just consciously dismissed it every time I saw it. At first the thoughts about it were passive: "You don't have time." or "What nonsense!" But as time passed the thoughts about that still-unopened book became aggressive: "How *dare* Sandi give you a book of lies!" or "God *hates* books about the occult" or "God will hate *you* if you read it."

I don't know why I never moved the book, but I just started to avoid being around it. Oddly enough, I realized that I was angry at it. I was aggressively angry at a book I'd never read. One afternoon in a fit of disgust I decided it was time to get rid of it. Picking it up I thought to myself, "The author of this *#@?%#!* book is a *#@?%#!* liar. He's going to hell and wants to take you with him!!"

Wow! Where did that come from? Why would I think such a thing? I flipped the book over to the back cover where I read the author's bio: "Don Dickerman, an ordained Southern Baptist minister, has directed an evangelistic ministry to prisons since 1974."[28] Well, that explains it. "Of course, people in prison can have demons," I thought to myself, "And besides he's a Southern Baptist. How radical can he be?"

I wasn't sure I even believed in demons, really. I opened the cover and began to read.

Once I started, I couldn't put it down. It was both riveting and challenging. It seemed to ring true, but it was still counter-intuitive to my long-held theological believes - like when I first met Lee. My past theology held that Jesus doesn't heal in the modern world today. Yet, here I am walking around pain-free as proof that He does. "Maybe there's something to this 'demon' thing, too." I thought to myself.

I took a moment to ask God to tell me if this was something I should embrace or run from. I read on.

By chapter six I was more than intrigued as I started reading a list of "Some Things Demons Don't Like." The first one on the list made perfectly logical sense:

"#1-Demons don't like the name of Jesus Christ."

The second item raised the hair on the back of my neck:

"#2-Demons cannot stand praise music."[29]

I immediately thought of my worship night experiences with Joe and Kim. Could my unexplained anger at the loud worship music be somehow related to demons? I read on.

By the time I finished the book, I was convinced that there was something to this. I didn't know exactly what, but I needed to find out. In spite of rising fear and uncertainty, I picked up the phone.

"Sandi?" I asked as she answered, "What do I do now?"

She gave me the contact information for Don Dickerman Ministries and encouraged me to act quickly before I changed my mind or "the demons talk you out of it." Then she quipped with dead-seriousness in her voice: "What do you have to loose but a few demons?"

PIG SHOWDOWN

"How stupid are you, Camille? This #@?%#! son of a #@?%#! can't help you. He can't help himself. He's a #@?%#! liar. You're going to regret this. He won't *deliver* you. Demons aren't real. This is a front for a #@?%#! cult, and you just opened the door and walked right in. You're gonna get exactly what you #@?%#! deserve!! . . . "

This was the barrage of unspoken thought going on in my head as I crossed the threshold and met Billy, ex-cop turned deliverance counselor. He was a man of robust stature with a gentle, but commanding presence. If the thoughts in my head had anything to do with it, I would not like him.

Jittery and anxious, I took my seat on Billy's couch as the ambush of my thoughts became viler toward this man. In spite of the onslaught of uncontrollable defamation going on in my head, I tried to redirect my thoughts and focus on what Billy was telling me.

"This is a truth encounter, not a power encounter . . . I'll ask you questions and your answers will come as thoughts or visual images. Just tell me whatever you hear or see or feel. Sometimes the demons will threaten you or talk trash about me. Just tell me. I won't expose you or embarrass you. You're safe with me. Whatever you're thinking or feeling? I want to know."

"No, you don't!" I thought to myself, wondering what he would really think if I spoke my thoughts out loud. For the time being, I kept my encroaching thoughts to myself and tried to focus.

Billy reminded me that demons can only enter in or torment us when we give them permission to do so through "open doorways." Some of these we open ourselves through unforgiveness, unrepentant sin, trauma, soul ties, or disobedience. Others have been opened for us as a result of the sins of our generational ancestors. The key, he explained, is to identify the open doors and close them. Once the demons no longer have permission to stay, they must leave when commanded to do so under the authority of Jesus' name.

I started to feel nauseated. "Billy," I interrupted, "Do you have a trash can in here?" He pointed to the left of the couch as I reached to move it closer to me. His look of inquiry prompted me to explain that I was feeling queasy. "Let's take care of that," he responded nonchalantly and addressed the demons directly:

"Every demon power that is causing Camille to feel nauseated right now, you must stop it now in the name of Jesus. This is my house; therefore it is Christ's house. Stop the nausea. In the name of Jesus, be still."

Immediately, the nausea and dizziness ceased, and Billy had my undivided attention. At that moment I *knew* this demon thing was real. They were inside of me. And I wanted them out.

Now, fully convinced that my participation was required to complete that task, I gave voice to the thoughts in my head without regard to social convention. What I thought, I said. Billy and I worked our way through the questionnaire that I had filled out in advance of my coming. We talked through all possible areas of permission. At each step, he walked me through prayers of forgiveness and repentance. We talked out issues of trust and unforgiveness. It felt freeing to talk openly about the fear, rejection, and insecurity that I'd been repressing for decades. But the thoughts in my head were increasing their "smack" talk. Several hours later, with all my doorways closed and permission canceled, Billy got down to business.

PIGS ON TRIAL

"When I start this thing," Billy began, "it's going to be a lot like a courtroom. I'm going to take the demons to *God's* courtroom. He will be their judge. I'll be your defense attorney today. I'm going to represent you against the evidence of the accuser. I'm going to play prosecutor. I'm going to put the demons on the witness stand, and I am going to interrogate them. I want to know who the demons are by name. Then I want to know what they do. What their function is in your life and where they are in your body. You just have to be a vessel. What you hear? Give it to me."

I was more excited than trepidatious at this point. In addition to the nausea that had arisen early in the session, I had also experienced the initial onset of a migraine aura. To both of these manifestations, Billy had spoken with authority to the demons and the symptoms had ceased immediately. Somehow, I *knew* this was real. Never before had I been able to stop the onset of a migraine once the aura had begun! The demons were in me, and Billy was the man to help me be free of them.

Billy placed the demons under the authority of Jesus and began to call them out. "I now separate the highest-ranking demon prince present. Highest-ranking demon, prince of the overall kingdom, come forward now. Bend your knee before Jehovah God and bend your knee before Camille in whom He resides. Highest-ranking demon prince, come forward and identify yourself by name. Who are you? Give Camille your name."

Nothing happened.

"Just tell me what you hear," Billy prompted me.

I listened. Everything had gone quiet, including the thoughts in my head. "Nothing. I hear the fan in the hall."

Billy explained that there must still be an open permission because "they (the demons) have been talking at you all morning and now they're silent."

Billy prayed, "Holy Spirit, will you show Camille . . ."

As we sat there waiting in utter silence I began to see in my mind's eye the manifestation of a recurring nightmare I'd had all of my adult life. I described it to Billy in detail. The horrific climax of the dream always involved the diminishing of my strength as I tried to keep closed the front door of my childhood home behind which "evil" was trying to gain entrance. I would always awaken in fear and panic just as the door was crashing in on me.

"Ask the Holy Spirit to open the door for you. Tell me who you see." I was shocked when the Holy Spirit showed me the "evil" behind the door. With gentle prompting, Billy spoke, "*That's* who you need to forgive."

I was absolutely stunned by this revelation. It made perfect sense in hindsight, but I had no idea that I had actually been holding this person in unforgiveness for all these years. When I confessed my unforgiveness and asked the Lord to forgive me, the demons started spilling their guts.

Billy began to call them out one-by-one, asking for their name, their function, and their permission. I simply listened to the thoughts that rose up in my mind and spoke them out. It was a bizarre experience. The pitch and timbre of my voice changed in response to these thoughts, sometimes my voice sounded sarcastic or defensive, sometime angry and violent. I even spoke and spelled the names of these demons - names I could hardly pronounce, let alone spell.

With each bit of information Billy collected from the demons, he used it against them to gain more incriminating information. After seventeen years of experience, Billy had learned that certain demons tend to run in packs. If one is present, so will his "buddies" be. He called them all out by name.

I learned through this experience that demons apparently organize themselves in hierarchical fashion with a "prince" at the top of the pack. With each question asked and answered, the demons gave Billy clues to the puzzle, and

Billy knew when he was finally talking to the top demon. The demon prince was defiantly denying his existence and refusing to give his name, when Billy called him by name: "It's a bad day for you, (Name)[30], isn't it?" The demon's response was delayed, almost inaudible, and clearly defeated, "Yes."

And then Billy began to wrap things up. He called them all to attention according to their names, hierarchical positions and functions. He ordered them to put back what they had destroyed - both physically and mentally and *"set the house in order."*[31] Fourteen demons had been identified by name and ranged in function from fear, migraines, doubt, confusion, control, unbelief, and one whose sole job it was to make me feel unloved. Can you belief that?

As Billy gave the demons time to "pack up and set things right" I began to see a picture in my mind's eye. Eventually, I would paint it on canvas. From my perspective, I was looking out from behind prison bars, only the "bars" seemed to be a cross-section view of walls that were regularly spaced in front of me, some thicker than others. When I heard Billy give the final command for the demons to leave, I heard him say, "And let Camille know when you're gone."

Immediately, I saw what looked like a ballistics test being played out in my mind - like a bullet being fired in slow motion into those prison-bar walls. As the bullet moved from left to right with lightning speed, each wall sequentially exploded into shattered pieces and disappeared. It was fast and furious and, when the last wall fell, my mind's eye was flooded with what seemed like an ocean of electrifying, life-giving, blue light that engulfed me with overwhelming love.

I exuberantly exclaimed, "Billy, I'm free!"

"Yes, darlin'. You are."

JOY IN THE VICTORY

Well if you're still reading this account, I applaud you for making it through my deliverance testimony! I must confess that it sounds "off the wall" to me every time I share it. And it seems so odd to see it set in black and white print. But I'm trusting the Holy Spirit to help you process it through his filter of love. He longs for his children to be free from demonic oppression.

The enemy's assignment as described in Scripture is to *"steal, kill, and destroy"*[32] - and that includes destroying our peace. But Jesus' mission here on earth is to *"set the captives free."*[33] What we keep hidden in the dark will inevitably oppress us. What we bring into the light can't defeat us. This is, quite literally, what Jesus meant when he declared that "*The Truth* (of who He is) *will set you free."*[34] Jesus defeated death when he rose from the grave, including all the powers of darkness that are hell-bend on destroying us all. Jesus is our protection against Satan and his minions, and Jesus has given us authority to enforce our victory in his name.

I smile in my spirit when I remember that life-changing day in Billy's office. "What just happened?" I asked him among my joyful tears and giddy laughter. I was free, and Billy was pumped up like an excited athlete retelling the story of his victory.

"Wasn't that cool - how everything broke loose all of a sudden? Nothing was happening, and then we start taking you through those confessions. 'Holy Spirit, show her where it started.' And, boy, I hit on that rejection thing and it exploded!"

Then he gave me a warning, explaining that from this point forward it would be up to me to enforce my own freedom, "We cast them out, but there's plenty more demons out there that want to take their place." He cautioned further: "They're going to come after you. And what you need to learn is that every thought that comes to your mind on any given day is from one of two spirits - either the Holy Spirit of God or some unholy spirit. You have to decide whether or not you're going to let them in."

Now I don't go around looking for demons everywhere, but I am a strict gatekeeper of my thoughts. I discovered supernatural, God-given peace at the moment of my deliverance, and I will not allow it to be compromised or violated. When I'm confronted with a thought that threatens to negate my peace, whether my own thought or one spoken to me, I ask myself this simple question, "Would Jesus say that to me?" If I know in my spirit that Jesus would never say that to me, then I reject the thought as a lie of the enemy and refuse it outright. It's only when I believe their lies that the demons have power over me. I no longer stoop to their trickery!

I apply this same process to the people I spend time with and the choices I make about entertainment options - what books I read, movies I watch, and activities in which I partake. I enjoy being around people who speak with life-affirming optimism, and I seek to eliminate all negativity from my vocabulary. Scripture declares that *"Death and life are in the power of the tongue."*[35] I choose life-giving optimism.

Of course, at times, I make unwise choices, allow in unholy thoughts or speak words that are not life-affirming. But as soon as I realize that my peace has been compromised, I confess it to the Lord, ask and receive His forgiveness, cancel the permission, and then command to leave any demon who gained entry through that open doorway. My peace always returns. "If in doubt, cast it out!"[36]

Five years has now passed since I sat there in Billy's office luxuriating in the aftermath of my newly-discovered freedom. I knew in that moment that I would never be the same. Something had changed - dramatically. The constant barrage of condemning demonic thoughts that had plagued me my whole life ceased in that moment, as did my battle with debilitating fear, depression, migraines, and chronic intestinal disorders. When the enemy retreated, Truth took hold of my heart, and then, I knew in my spirit with radical, undeniable certainty: *I am lovable*!

CHAPTER 8:

PARADIGM SHIFT

THERE'S ALWAYS A 'BUT . . .'

In the aftermath of my physical healing and deliverance experience, I became fully convinced that what I read in the pages of Scripture has more direct application to the modern world I live in than mainstream Bible scholars and preachers seem to give credence. I *know* that Jesus still heals. I *know* he still has authority over demons. I no longer have to have faith to believe it's true. I *know* it's true.

I began to read my Bible with an underlying question in the forefront of mind: What else have I been taught to overlook or dismiss?

Jesus talked about demons. He talked about them a lot. On occasion, Jesus talked directly to the demons, just like Billy did with the demons who were oppressing me. Jesus cast them out of people. He attributed sicknesses to them. He hated them for oppressing the very people he came to set free. And he demonstrated that he does, indeed, have that authority.

Demons still oppress, but Jesus still has the power and authority to set us free. That hasn't changed.

What has changed is the mindset of our post-modern, western culture. We have turned the realm of the demonic into entertainment. With every horror movie or sex-violence-language movie we watch in spite of the rating, we desensitize ourselves. When our viewing participation contributes to the popularity of competitive reality television, we are saying it's OK to destroy the human spirit through negative criticism and back-stabbing manipulation. And when we believe the television commercials or magazine ads that bait us into believing we're not beautiful enough, happy enough, or secure enough, we are *choosing* to believe the demonic lies that oppress us.

Our churches should be a respite from our oppression-tolerant culture, but sadly most are not. Many have become houses of legalism or indifference rather than beacons of Spirit-empowering freedom. For fifty-two years I was taught to read my Bible through a lens of limitation: "Feel free to rejoice in the miraculous healings of Jesus and celebrate the supernatural power of the Holy Spirit on the day of Pentecost, *but* it was only for the apostles, not for us today."

There was always a "but . . ." and that "but" led me straight into demonic oppression. If I limit the miraculous to first century Christianity, then I become impotent against my twenty-first century enemy. What is *super*natural to us, from our human perspective, is simply God's natural.

AN INVITATION TO DANCE

We were all gathered around the living room in our customary style at

IN JOY!

Joe and Kim's worship night. It was a few weeks after my deliverance experience, and I was seated on the floor with my back against the couch. Joe opened in prayer and as he turned on the worship music, he encouraged us, "Ask Jesus to tell you what's on his heart for you tonight."

Normally annoyed and angered by the loud volume of Joe's music, that night I felt as if I simply melted into it. I smiled to myself knowing that the demons were no longer provoking me to anger. I shifted into the mindset of worship, focusing on a simple truth with a grateful heart: "Jesus loves me."

It's hard to put into words what I experienced that night. Some would tell me later that it was an "open vision." Others called it an "awake dream." In 2 Corinthians, the apostle Paul talks about being "*caught up into Paradise - whether in the body or out of the body I do not know, God knows.*"[37] Whatever you call it, for me, it was tangible and very real.

As I began to worship that night, I found myself in a country-western bar. Obviously, I was sitting on the floor in Joe's living room, but in my mind's eye I was sitting alone at a table in a smoke-filled, Texas-style honky tonk with a wood-plank dance floor, twangy guitars, and dim lighting. My heart was heavy with isolation as I sat there, head bowed, more aware of the clanking of bar glasses and the hustle of the barkeep than the dancing going around me. Assuming that I would never be asked to dance, I was startled to see a set of alligator cowboy boots step into my lowered vision.

The owner of those boots whispered gently as he extended his hand in invitation, "Come dance with me." I could hear a smile in his voice as I placed my hand in his and raised my gaze to meet his. In that moment, as I yielded to his touch, our location changed.

All the trappings of the honky tonk disappeared, and I found myself in an open meadow of such beauty that I cannot adequately describe it. I wasn't just imagining this place. I was there. I could smell its deliciousness, feel its "gloriousness," and soak in the wonderment of colors I had never seen before. I could hear strains of music in the distance beyond a grassy knoll, but I could not identify its source and had no frame of reference with which to experience it. It was an altogether different kind of music.

I turned to the mysterious stranger who still held my hand, and stood amazed at his transformation. No longer identified with cowboy attire and no longer a stranger, Jesus stood before me. He was dressed in elegant linen - a white, collar-less, knee-length tunic over white slacks with strapped sandals on his feet. His clothing did not glow or look like lightening. He was just Jesus in human form holding my hand and waiting for me to catch up to the experience. In my moment of recognition, he leaned his head back and let out a belly-laugh of joy. No doubt, he was delighting in the revelation I was experiencing.

"What is this place?" I asked with astonishment.

With the question unanswered and a twinkle in his eye, he leaned in as if he were going to reveal a precious secret and whispered in my ear, "Let's dance."

The music that came from the distance began to advance toward us. I could actually *see* the music as it engulfed us like a breeze. Lost in the blue-eyed gaze of my Savior, I began to dance to his lead - not the slow dance of a sensual nature, but one of child-like delight. We laughed out loud, spun around in intoxicating dizziness, and delighted in each other's joy. His eyes sparkled and his laugh was irresistibly contagious. This was no angry God of condemnation and judgment. This was the overwhelming love of Jesus in tangible form.

As we danced, I seemed to be aware of a crowd watching us - people or angels, I do not know - I could not see them. I could only feel them as their love engulfed us. But Jesus only had eyes for me. I was the focus of all his attention. I never felt more loved, and in that moment I became aware that *my* appearance, too, had changed.

My shortly-cropped hair style was now shoulder length, blowing gently in the breeze from underneath a simple crown of white flowers. I felt the grass tickle my now bare feet and, looking down, realized that I was wearing a white dress of elegant simplicity with a flowing hem line that swayed in response to my movements. A sprouting of wildflowers spread from my feet outward until the entire meadow was spectacularly arrayed in colorful blooms. I had become a bride adorned for her beloved. In that moment, I fell head-over-heals in love with the one who invited me to the dance, and I knew that he was head-over-heals in love with me.

One final spin and Jesus began to retreat. He did not turn his back on me. He simply began to move away. "You're leaving?" I asked without a hint of rejection, fear or reproof. He laughed with reassuring joy, "Keep dancing! I'll be back again when the tempo changes." With that, I continued to dance and spin my way right back into Joe and Kim's living room.

There was a moment of readjustment as I relished the aftermath of my encounter with Jesus and became reoriented to my physical surroundings. The worship music was playing a final refrain and no one around me seemed to have noticed that I had been "gone." But as Joe began to transition us out of our worship time he asked, "Did anyone have an unusual experience tonight during worship?" He then explained that he felt the Lord's prompting to extend the music about thirty minutes beyond what he had planned.

I shared my experience with the group and relished the fact that Jesus had supernaturally orchestrated events simply because he wanted to spend over an hour of uninterrupted time dancing with me. In that experience I learned something about myself: Not only am I lovable; I am deeply loved.

CAN'T TAKE CREDIT

My journey from oppressive bondage into Spirit-empowered freedom began by way of supernatural healing. My physical healing opened the door to the experiences of abiding, worship and freedom, and I was determined to take my newly-found freedom for a spin!

I was embarking upon a new journey and had no idea where it would lead. But what I knew for sure was that deep transformation was occurring in my spirit. It was radical and freeing, but at the same time "restless." My spirit was becoming increasingly restless, but not in the sense of being unsettled or anxious. I simply could not find a place of intellectual rest as I tried to reconcile my life's experience of performance-based religion with what I was now experiencing. This was something entirely different.

> I had done nothing to earn my physical healing. I had not sought out my encounter with Lee nor even offered a sliver of faith in supernatural healing. And, yet, God healed me.
>
> I had done nothing to warrant the rejection and opposition of my church family in the aftermath of my healing. I simply told my story. And, yet, God sent me to Pastor David who encouraged me to abide.
>
> I was unable to move myself beyond fear and rejection as I repeatedly declined Amy's invitations to meet Joe and Kim. And, yet, God used Rosemary to make that connection for me.
>
> I contributed nothing significant to the worship experience at Joe and Kim's. And, yet, God used the genuine, Spirit-filled worship of others to begin gently breaking through my walls of resistance.
>
> I outright rejected Sandi's account of her experience with the demonic realm - much like my church family had done to me. Her story was too radical for me. And, yet, God moved me beyond my prejudice and led me to Billy.

I did nothing to earn my freedom from demonic oppression. If the truth be told, I showed up at Billy's on a dare from Sandi with the determination to prove them both wrong. And, yet, God surprised me with radical freedom.

I did nothing to earn God's love. And, yet, he came to dance with me. For the first time in my life at the age of 52 and with a lifetime of evidence to the contrary, I knew that I was lovable. At that moment in time I could not have explained how I knew, I just knew. It was as if God by-passed my fifty-two years of intellectual reasoning and flawed logic by simply depositing that truth directly into my spirit during a life-altering dance.

As I take a moment to read back over this list of God-initiated events in my life I feel an often-quoted Scripture rising up in my spirit: *"Apart from me,"* Jesus said, *"you can do nothing."*[38] At the same time, the moniker "Jehovah Sneaky" is making me laugh. Noted Christian author Graham Cooke uses this phrase to describe how God (Jehovah) often catches us unaware.

How thankful I am! God did not leave me in my state of unforgiveness and oppression, floundering to relate to him only through performance-oriented, religious regimens. Jehovah Sneaky stepped in and orchestrated each and every one of these path-correcting encounters.

God initiates and our job is to respond. Sometimes we respond with great faith and confidence. Sometimes our response is to simply show up - to walk through the door God opens before us. I believe that when I was at my weakest, God knew that I was not able to respond with unshakable faith (or any level of faith, at all), so he initiated his desires for me through Lee, Amy, Rosemary, Joe, Kim, Sandi, Billy and countless others. God initiated and they responded on my behalf. How awesome is that?

Unknown to me at the time, the next move of God in my life would take more than one person's influence. It would require the influence of 25,000 believers!

IT FELT FAMILIAR

I was struggling more and more to relate to the people at my home church as I began to reevaluate my relationship with Jesus through the filters of healing and deliverance. If the folks at my church were reluctant to accept my story of supernatural healing, how would they react to my testimony of freedom from demonic oppression? Or to a supernatural dance with Jesus? I continued to attend but felt myself withdrawing from personal interactions. The God I met through healing and freedom now seemed so much bigger than the doctrine-limited God of my home church. My restless spirit longed for more.

"It's called *Habitation*," she explained as she extended an invitation for me to join her. "Richard and I went last month, and it was amazing! You have to come with us."

In her post-deliverance restlessness, my friend Sandi was searching for answers, too. She was excited about this monthly church service she'd discovered, and I readily accepted her invitation. I had no idea at the time that Jehovah Sneaky was up to something big.

We pulled into the church parking lot the following Sunday evening, and my heart sank with instant disappointment. It was a mega church - one of those massive churches with too many people, a grand building, and a parking lot that rivals those of popular shopping malls. Although I had no personal experience with them, I held a stereotypical bias against mega churches. Surely there was something amiss about that many people devoted to a single pastor and that much money being "tithed" into one location. I had overtones of cult, misuse, and superficiality built into my prejudice against them. Besides, I had enough trouble with the rejection of 2,700 people, let alone 25,000 of them. Needless to say, I was wary as we made our way across the parking lot and into the building.

Walking through the fashionable lobby I had an unexpected, yet familiar, thought cross my mind: *Do you trust me?* Before I had time to react to this probing thought, we were greeted by an usher at the door of the worship center. In similar fashion to my first experience at Lee's church, worship was already underway. As we stepped into the darkened auditorium God literally took my breath away.

I gasped.

Startled by my reaction Sandi turned and asked, "Are you OK?" Speechless, I nodded in the affirmative as the usher led us to our seats and gentle tears began to well up and roll down my cheeks. I *felt* it. It was in the air. It was supernatural. And, surprisingly, it was familiar.

It was the same weightiness in the air that I had experienced so tangibly in my bedroom on the morning of my healing - like smelling someone's perfume lingering in the air long after they've left the room. Only here in this darkened auditorium with thousands of worshiping believers, it was not lingering. It was thickening. The atmosphere's tangible weightiness rested on me with supernatural Presence, and I *heard* deep in my spirit:

These people will show you the Truth.

As the service transitioned out of the worship portion of the service, a pastor made his way through the musicians toward the center of the platform. "Can you feel him?" he asked the congregation. "The Holy Spirit is here with us tonight. Can you feel him?" A momentary hush fell across the room as everyone, myself included, savored the experience. Then as quickly as the hush fell it exploded into a spontaneous recapitulation of praise and worship. I took it all in with amazement.

The pastor gave a message that night that was theology-shifting for me. I believed in a triune God, three in one - God the Father, Jesus the Son, and the Holy Spirit. I had been taught that the Holy Spirit's role in our culture today is limited to convicting us of sin and leading us to salvation in Jesus. All true. But this pastor was unashamedly declaring that the supernatural workings of the Holy Spirit are not limited to first-century Christianity. I was astonished. Then I was blown away.

The Testimonial portion of their service followed the pastor's message. One after another, the pastor interviewed people who, just like me, told stories of their supernatural healings. There was no evidence of overt emotionalism or theatrics. In fact, these stories did not even seem unusual to them. They expected the Holy Spirit to heal and minister on their behalf. This was a radical paradigm shift for me - a church that was not ashamed or afraid of the Holy Spirit! They celebrated him equally with God the Father and Jesus the Son.

Jehovah Sneaky had snuck up on me again! Without a doubt, I knew that evening's experience had been another God-orchestrated path correction. I felt it deep in my spirit. At some point during the course of the evening, my restlessness had given way to anticipation. God was up to something new, and I was excited to partner with Him. "Yes, Lord, I trust you to show me the Truth."

I just never believed he would use a mega church to do it.

TO MEGA OR NOT TO MEGA

I did not immediately jump ship and join this new church, but I was drawn to it. I began to attend their Saturday night services with increasing regularity. I couldn't seem to let go of the conviction that there was spiritual truth to be found here - truth that would settle my restless spirit.

Located in the Dallas-Fort Worth area, the church's pastor described the multi-location church not as charismatic or Pentecostal, but "Spirit-empowered."

Week after week the lead pastor unpacked the Scriptures through a theological lens that challenged many of my long-held beliefs. With each paradigm-shifting revelation came internal conflict. And more often than not, the point of challenge had to do with the ministry of the Holy Spirit.

For a season I attended this new church on Saturday nights and my own church on Sunday mornings. And more and more I struggled with which theological viewpoint to embrace. Deep in my spirit I wanted to explore the Spirit-empowered lifestyle, but to fully embrace that theology left me feeling as if I would be betraying a lifetime of learning. I asked the Lord to give me direction.

Several weeks later as I was reading through 1 Thessalonians, I reread what had become for me a "life" verse:

> *"Rejoice always, pray continually, give thanks in all circumstances; for this is God's will for you in Christ Jesus."* (1 Thessalonians 5:16-18, NIV)

Memorized and recalled endlessly throughout my years of physical pain, this verse of Scripture was deeply personal. It brought me comfort and reassurance, reminding me that God was in the midst of my circumstances with me, and I could rejoice in that. Because of my familiarity with this verse I rarely read it in its context, but on this day the verses immediately following jumped off the page as I read:

> *"Do not quench the [Holy] Spirit. Do not despise prophesies, but test every thing, hold fast what is good. Abstain from every form of evil."* (1 Thessalonians 5:19-22, ESV)

There was my answer. God had spoken through Scripture, and I felt excitement rise up inside of me. From that day forward, I went in search of the Holy Spirit with confidence. This Scripture, in essence, gave me permission to explore or "test" theological truths with the certainty that the Lord would guide me into Truth.

I embraced my new church as the gateway through which I would soon discover a personal, spirit-to-Spirit friendship with the Holy Spirit.

PARADIGM SHIFT

CHAPTER 9:

SPIRIT-EMPOWERED LIVING

THREE IS BETTER THAN ONE

"Three baptisms? Are you serious?"

The sermon series was entitled "The God I Never Knew," and the pastor was claiming that there are Scriptural references to verify three baptism events in the life of a Jesus-follower. This was shocking to me. I only had experience with water baptism.

I was baptized with water at the age of eight when I invited Jesus into my heart to be my Savior. I had been taught to read Biblical references about the Holy Spirit baptism through the lens of cessationist theology. It was for first-century believers, not modern-day believers. But this pastor was stating matter-of-factly that there are three baptisms, all of which I can experience personally.

This was spirit-awakening revelation to me as I processed all he was saying. I bought a copy of his book, *The God I Never Knew,* and couldn't put it down. This was radical! There are three baptisms, and I can have a personal relationship with the Holy Spirit? I didn't know exactly what it would look or feel like, but I wanted it.

I recommend this book to you for a more thorough explanation, but I don't want to keep you in the dark. Here's a synopsis of the three baptisms in order of their most common sequence in Scripture. Pay attention to the nouns in these statements because they tell whose doing the baptism:

SALVATION: The Holy Spirit baptizes us into Jesus - When we profess our faith in Jesus as Lord, the Holy Spirit baptizes us into the body of Christ. At that point we are saved:

> *"For by one Spirit we were all baptized into one body" (the church)."* (1 Corinthians 12:13, NASB)

WATER: Disciples baptize us into water - This is not just an outward act of obedience or a religious rite of passage. This is the burial of our old nature and the establishment of our new nature. It is a supernatural exchange:

> *"We were buried therefore with him (Jesus) by baptism unto death, in order that, just as Christ was raised from the dead by the glory of the Father, we too might walk in newness of life."* (Romans 6:4, ESV)

SPIRIT: Jesus baptizes us into the Holy Spirit - After we receive our salvation and our new nature we are ready to receive our Spirit empowerment.

John the Baptist tells us that it is Jesus who initiates:

> "I (John) baptize you with water for repentance. But after me comes one who is more powerful than I, whose sandals I am not worthy to carry. He (Jesus) will baptize with the Holy Spirit and with fire." (Matthew 3:11, NIV)

Up until my deliverance experience at the age of 52, I carried within me a debilitating fear of fire, the aftermath of surviving a traumatic house fire at the age of six. Throughout my life I had found comfort (relief, really) in the teaching that this "Spirit" baptism was only for the first-century apostles. I certainly had no interest in being baptized with fire! But I was now on a journey of discovery and so began to test this new theology through prayer and Scripture.

The more I read on the subject and the more teaching I received through my church's classes on the subject, the more peace I had in my spirit.

"Jesus, I want this, too."

My prayer was genuine. Just like when, as an act of faith, I had asked Jesus into my heart at the age of eight, I asked Jesus to baptize me into the Holy Spirit.

"But go easy on the fire part. OK, Lord?"

I waited several moments in expectation.

Nothing happened. No fire or whirling winds. No odd languages or bizarre behavior emerged. Nothing out of the ordinary. "Hum," I thought to myself as I wondered exactly what I had been expecting.

Several days went by as I continually asked the Lord, "Will you please baptize me into the Holy Spirit?" It became quite urgent in my spirit, and I couldn't let go of it. I wanted to experience what so many at church were talking about. They had it, and I wanted it. "Lord, *please*, will you please let me experience it, too?"

I think Jehovah Sneaky was laughing with Jesus when, at that moment of pleading, I heard in my spirit:

I already have.

Startled by such an odd thought, I responded back with this thought, "You already have what?"

Baptized you into the Holy Spirit.

"You did?"

Yep.

"When?"

Immediately, I remembered my experience in Billy's office at the end of my deliverance session. Billy had given the demons the command to leave and my mind's eye had been flooded with electrifying, life-giving, blue light that overwhelmed me with love and supernatural peace.

Giggling with wonderment as the revelation washed over me, I laughed out loud: "The Holy Spirit is blue?"

V.I.P. SEATING

I love that Jesus baptized me into the Holy Spirit without me realizing that's what had happened. He bypassed all my stereotyped notions of emotionalism and odd-for-God behavior. With my freedom from demonic oppression had come Spirit empowerment; and, once again, I hadn't done anything to earn it or deserve it. But now that I had it, I wanted to understand what it meant to live a Spirit-filled lifestyle.

I had so many questions but no personal connection with anyone whom I felt comfortable asking. Although I had been attending my new church for several months, I was becoming increasingly frustrated at my inability to make a personal connection with someone who could help me unlock the mysteries of Spirit-filled living. In spite of the thousands of people around me every Sunday morning, I was becoming more and more isolated and frustrated.

"Lord, I can't do this anymore!" I cried out to him in child-like pouting. "I'm not going back."

But I did anyway. The following Sunday, as was my custom, I entered the worship center early and made my way down to the front, center section. But I was turned away several times:

"These seats are reserved today." "You can't sit here." "Sorry, if you're not part of . . ."

Apparently, a special event was occurring that day and these folks made it pretty clear that I was not part of it. In actuality, their words were not harshly delivered, at all. They had simply touched the rejection wounds in my spirit. Tears began to well up, "Lord, I *knew* I shouldn't have come back."

As I turned to make my way back up the aisle toward the exit my attention was drawn to an elderly woman sitting on the aisle. She waved her hand to get my attention. As I approached and knelt down to talk with her, she pointed to the center of her aisle and said, "Honey, God saved that seat for you. Next to that lady right there."

I didn't think much of it in that moment, but it derailed my determination to leave. I thanked her and made my way toward the indicated seat.

"Is this seat taken?" I asked the woman sitting next to my "reserved" seat.

"No. Please join me. I'm Sherrie."

"It's nice to meet you. I'm Camille. The lady at the end of the aisle told me that God saved this seat for me."

She laughed, "Well, then it's *really* nice to meet you!"

As we began to engage in typical chit-chat, I shifted my weight to the edge of the seat and was sitting with my back toward the aisle from which I had entered. I was unaware that another lady was approaching us until she taped me on the shoulder. I turned toward her.

"Is this seat available?" she asked.

"Yes. Come join us. I'm Camille and this is Sherrie. We were just getting acquainted."

"I'm Jennifer. This may sound strange, but the lady at the end of the aisle told me that God saved *this* seat for me."

Sherrie and I made eye contact and began to laugh with amazement as we filled Jennifer in on our secret. God was certainly in that moment when he purposefully connected us together. Sherrie spontaneously extended an invitation, "Come join me next week in the Prayer Tools class. We meet at the 9:00 hour and the teaching is amazing. I'll look for you there."

As we began to explore our friendship over the next few weeks, we learned that our connectivity had surely been a divinely-orchestrated answer to each of our individual prayers. Sherrie was ten years my senior and experienced in the ways of Spirit-filled living. Although married, she had been attending church alone each week. Jennifer, five years my junior, was a new believer in Jesus and trying to find her way, as well.

There is no doubt in my mind. God himself arranged for us to meet so he could knit us together in a season of friendship. We all felt the divine nature of it. For me, this friendship was more than just connectivity. Through Sherrie and Jennifer the Lord showed me that the fear of rejection has no place in God-ordained relationships. He was teaching me how to trust.

And because of Sherrie's initial invitation to join her in the Prayer Tools class, I discovered a whole array of classes that were available to me. I absorbed them all - classes on prayer, freedom, the nature of God, growing in the Spirit, healing, spiritual gifts, identity development, financial freedom, worship, and so many more! These amazing classes are taught by pastors and professors from my church and an accredited university under its umbrella. These leaders had become my treasure-trove of Spirit-filled mentors.

OVERCOMING LOGIC AND REASON

As I began to explore the world of Spirit-empowered living, I realized more and more that I had some major hurdles of learned, "performance" Christianity to overcome. And the biggest hurdle to start was overcoming logic and reason.

The church and home culture I grew up in put a major emphasis on the pursuit of learning and intellectualism. Study of the Bible had been my primary source of connectivity with God. My reasoning proposed that if I can understand God, I can connect to him. Prayer, for me, had always been a means for testing and re-evaluating my logic and reasoning about God. If answers to prayer did not come, I'd go back and study more. Surely, I was smart enough to figure out how to pray the right prayer. Do you see the problem? I would never be smart enough because humans cannot effectively evaluate spiritual matters through head knowledge.

Adam and Eve learned this the hard way.

The Bible tells us that the habitation of Eden was full of all the abundance of God's goodness. With amazing things to eat without toil or preparation and with no predators to fear, Adam and Eve luxuriated in their spiritual connection with their Creator. They spoke and walked with him among the garden "*in the cool of the day.*"[39] They were free to be who God intended them to be, to walk in spiritual connectedness with the Creator himself. It was an environment rich with potential for spiritual growth. But they had a choice to make.

Among all the good gifts in the garden, God placed only one restriction. "*Don't eat from this tree.*"[40] He called it the "*tree of the knowledge of good and evil,*" and he placed it in proximity to another tree called the "*tree of life.*" Both were located together in the middle of the garden as a focal point - a daily choice.

I believe Adam and Eve ate continually from the unrestricted "*tree of life*" up until their fateful decision. I suspect that its fruit was deliciously addictive both in taste and spiritual connectivity to God. They were eating *life!*

But when they ate from the forbidden tree, they unplugged from the true source of life and chose knowledge instead. They unplugged from pure, life-giving, spirit-to-Spirit communication with God and plugged into themselves. They became their own source of life as they disconnected from Godly wisdom and revelation. From that point in history forward, the intellectual reason and logic of mankind has interrupted our communication with God, the true source of life-giving power.

In his book, *Think Differently Life Differently,* Bob Hamp likens it to disconnecting a computer from its power cable and relying only on its data cable:

"Data alone cannot sustain power, but if data is all that is available, you will try to draw power from it."[41]

I had spent decades trying to draw life from intellectual pursuits. I had learned to be good at religious activity but lacked spiritual connectivity. That's why Lee's way of "knowing" and Billy's confident resolve to enforce victory over unseen forces seemed so foreign to me. I had no logical arguments with which to evaluate them; and yet, I had personal experiences that were undeniable. I could not explain supernatural healing, but I knew I had experienced it. The same applied to freedom from demonic oppression, a supernatural dance and divinely-orchestrated friendships.

As I began to learn the ways of the Spirit I began to embrace the things I couldn't understand. I set them before the Lord for evaluation, "testing" each through Scripture and prayerful consideration. And because God leaves no stone unturned, he began to change my prayer life, too. I discovered a new way of communicating with God that unlocked my heart's desire.

CHAPTER 10:

TAPPING INTO POWER

PRAYING *WITH* GOD?

"Wow! These people even pray differently," I thought to myself as I sat in my first Prayer Tools class with Sherrie and Jennifer. I soaked it all in.

My experience with prayer up to that point in my life had been an ask-and-wait approach. God is sovereign. Therefore, his will is sovereign by default. As a believer in Jesus, I never doubted that I had permission to *"approach God's throne of grace with confidence"*[42] and *"make my requests known to God."*[43] I did it often - daily, in fact. But, in all honesty, I'd have to confess that I didn't think it really made much difference in the ultimate outcome. God was sovereign and would do want he wanted anyway, right?

With every prayer that began "Lord, if it be your will . . ," I placated any future disappointment with the knowledge-based belief that God was in control and knows what's best for me. This was the cycle of prayer that ultimately seemed to confirm my belief that God loved me but not enough to heal me. I determined that if God's will required me to live in physical pain then I would accept my fate as being the best I deserved (a demonic lie) and live it out with religious stoicism.

So, as I sat in the Prayer Tools class, the instructor captured my attention when she posed a paradigm-shifting question:

"Why would you choose to pray *to* God when you can pray *with* God?"

I listened intently as she began to explain how we can "partner" in prayer with Jesus and the Holy Spirit to pray the prayers *they* are praying.

The Bible tells us that Jesus lived on the earth, defeated death on the cross, and rose from the dead. He then ascended back to God. So have you ever wondered what Jesus has been doing ever since then?

> *"Jesus Christ, who died - more than that, who was raised to life - is at the right hand of God and is also interceding for us."* (Romans 8:34, NIV)

> *"Because Jesus lives forever, he has a permanent priesthood. Therefore he is able to save completely those who come to God through him because he always lives to intercede for them."* (Hebrews 7:24-25, NIV)

If Jesus is forever saving us and interceding (praying) for us, what's the Holy Spirit's role in our prayers?

> *"The Spirit helps us in our weakness. We do not know what we ought to pray for, but the Spirit himself intercedes for us with wordless groans."* (Romans 8:26, NIV)

> *"When the Spirit of truth comes, he will guide you into all truth . . . He (Holy Spirit) will glorify me (Jesus), for he will take what is mine and declare it to you."* (John 16:13-14, ESV)

Jesus and the Holy Spirit are continually lifting up prayers on our behalf. God the Father, God the Son, and God the Spirit are always in complete agreement. It's a circle of prayer on our behalf and on behalf of what God is doing in the world around us. God makes his will and desires known to Jesus who begins to pray it into being. Jesus reveals it to the Holy Spirit so he can pray and extend an open invitation for us to join them. When we accept, the Holy Spirit makes Jesus' desires known to us, too, so that our prayers come from a place of complete agreement with God's heart. This virtually removes disappointment from our prayer life as we are no longer praying our own desires, but God's. How cool is that?

FINE TUNING MY RECEIVER

In the Prayer Tools classes over the following weeks, months and years, I learned more about my relationship with the Holy Spirit - how to listen and interact with him. He is not the distant, first-century-only God that I had been taught to be wary of. The Holy Spirit is alive, present, interactive, and completely accessible. He is enthusiastic, encouraging, and funny! He has opened up to me a spiritual world of awe and wonder. He calls out of me the best I can be - all God designed me to be. He has become my best friend, and it all started when I came into agreement with one spiritual truth: God still speaks to us today.

When Jesus baptized me into the Holy Spirit there in Billy's office, I was unaware of the significance of the moment. Unlike the apostles on the Day of Pentecost[44], I did not experience tongues of fire resting on me nor did I speak out in a language not my own. I was certainly giddy and light-hearted in that moment, but I had no idea at the time that Jesus had supernaturally plugged me into a new power source.

I've heard it likened to the process of radio reception. At any given time radio waves are bouncing through the air all around me. I can't see them or feel them. They have no effect on me at all. They are simply there. But if I want them to be accessible to me I need the proper equipment - a radio. Once obtained, I can use my radio to tune into the right frequency and pick up the signal. Fine-tuning on my part allows me to hear the radio signal at its greatest clarity.

In the same way, Jesus gave me my spiritual "radio" when I invited him into my heart at the age of eight and was baptized with water. He exchanged my old nature for his new nature, thus turning on the power to my spiritual "radio." I then spent decades struggling through Christian performance activities trying to hear the signal more clearly. It was not until Jesus baptized me into the Holy Spirit at the age of 52 that I began to experience a spirit-to-Spirit connection at the proper frequency.

SIX GLASSES OF LEMONADE

As I was practicing interactive prayer one Saturday morning, I asked, "Lord, what do you want to pray about?" I sat in silent expectation. When no answer came, I eventually opened my Bible and began to read. I cannot recall what I was reading at the time, but I was fully engrossed in the process when a bizarre thought popped into my head: *Six glasses of lemonade.*

I dismissed it as a random distraction and tried to refocus. No luck. Every time I began to read I kept "hearing" the same thought: *Six glasses of lemonade.* It was relentless - and annoying, really. Finally, it began to dawn on me, and I inquired sheepishly, "Lord, is that you?" The response was urgent:

Get up now and make six glasses of lemonade.

It was so urgent in my spirit that I headed toward the kitchen wondering how I was supposed to make lemonade, knowing that I had none of the necessary ingredients in my kitchen. "Should I go to the store, Lord?"

Make six glasses of lemonade now.

I obeyed in response to the implied immediacy. It felt foolish on my part, but I removed six glasses from the cabinet and filled them with ice and cold water. "What now?" I thought as I sheepishly looked in the refrigerator to see if lemons had miraculously appeared. I waited.

Stir the lemonade.

"Seriously? What's to stir?" I thought as I opened the kitchen drawer to retrieve a stirring utensil. I laughed out loud when I reached in the seldom-used drawer and saw a long-forgotten container of water-flavoring drops - and of course it was lemonade flavored! I was all on board at that point, "OK, Lord. What should I do now?"

IN JOY!

Take them to the front porch.

I put the glasses on a tray and carried them with me to the front porch where I sat down and waited. Ten minutes or so passed in silence, and I was feeling pretty silly. My neighborhood was unusually quiet for a beautiful summer Saturday. I waited - for *what* or *whom* I didn't know.

About the time I was ready to dismiss this experience as simply a misdirected thought, I heard a child's voice in the distance. Looking in that direction I saw two women and a young boy walking down the street toward me. They seemed a bit over-dressed for a Saturday morning stroll, but as they approached I called out to them, "Would you like some lemonade?" The women declined, but the boy said, "Mommy, can I have some?" She seemed uncertain and began to decline again. "It's free!" I assured them.

The young boy ran across the grass toward me in active pursuit of lemonade. He drank with child-like zeal and asked, "How did you know we were coming?" I smiled knowingly and said, "Jesus told me to expect you." He responded with amazement, "Really?"

"Do you know, Jesus?" I asked him as the two women cautiously approached and interrupted before the child could answer. I suspect that it was an intentional interruption of the conversation on their part, but I offered them lemonade as the child enthusiastically endorsed it, "Mommy! This is the best lemonade *ever!*" We all laughed, and they joined us.

One of the women explained that they were sharing their faith door-to-door and offered me some literature. I accepted it graciously as it showed me that we were not of the same spiritual or religious persuasion. As she nervously began her prepared presentation I was momentarily distracted by the thought, "Lord, why did you want six glasses?"

Immediately, the woman interrupted herself and with relief in her voice said, "Oh, here they come." I looked down the street to see a man and two children walking toward us as she explained, "That's my husband and two of our kids." I let loose a spontaneous burst of laughter. I did not mean to cause her an offense, but the look on her face told me I had done so.

With dawning realization I exclaimed enthusiastically, "They are four, five, and six!" She looked puzzled, thinking that I was trying to make out the age of her children as they approached. "No, I didn't mean that," I tried to explain. "Before you came I was praying in my living room, and I felt like Jesus told me to make and bring out six glasses of lemonade. I couldn't figure out why there were only three of you. But here comes four, five, and six!"

She did not seem pleased, at all. I, on the other hand, was lost in the joy and wonder of the experience as my new, young friend called out to the other children, "Free lemonade!" To their Dad's apparent irritation, they broke from his side and ran toward us as the accolades continued, "It's the best lemonade *ever*!" I laughed again out loud as the thought crossed my mind that if Jesus could turn water into wine, he could miraculously make my flavor-drop water into the "best ever!"

Responding to the body language of her impatient husband, the woman hurriedly began to herd the children back toward the street. The young boy responded in obedience but after a short distance turned and came running back across the yard. He asked breathlessly, "Can I come again and have more lemonade?" I hurriedly answered as I saw the woman coming back to retrieve him, "Of course. Just tell Jesus you want his lemonade, and he'll tell me to have it ready for you when you come back." As he was being dragged back into compliance, I heard him tell his mom with enthusiasm, "The lady said Jesus will make me lemonade, and I can come back!"

Pure joy rose up in my spirit. I don't know how the mom responded. I don't know the outcome of the story. But I knew in that moment that something supernatural had occurred. "What was that all about, Lord?" I asked as I sat on the porch and returned the young boy's enthusiastic wave from the back seat of the car. As his father gave me an angry look and pulled away from the curb, I heard unmistakably in my spirit:

I have big plans for that young boy.

I let the revelation wash over me in a S*elah*[45] moment. The Holy Spirit had just revealed to me what was on God's heart for a total stranger. Had I ignored a seemingly random thought and not obediently prepared those six glasses of lemonade, I would never have experienced the wonder of partnering with God in carrying out his plans. And from that experience, I learned that I can hear God's voice, and every act of faith in response further serves to fine-tune my receiver to the frequency of God's voice.

But most importantly, I learned that Jesus and the Holy Spirit love to answer the question, "Lord, what do you want to pray about today?" I've had many divine prayer assignments in the years following that amazing summer day, but that particular prayer assignment is special to me. Every time I recall the experience I stop for a moment to join Jesus and the Holy Spirit in praying out God's plans for that young boy who loved Jesus' "best EVER!" lemonade.

GIFTS? FOR ME?

With every new experience of the Holy Spirit I felt a growing hunger rise up in me. I was being introduced to the missing piece of the puzzle. The "God I never knew"[46] was revealing himself with greater frequency as I yielded to deeper revelation. The more I experienced, the more I wanted. I wanted to experience it all - including the mysterious gifts of the Spirit.

Having been taught my whole life that the gifts of the Spirit were only available to first-century believers, it had been easy for me to dismiss them as irrelevant to my personal experience with God. In the church culture from which I came, the gifts were rarely mentioned unless shrouded in mystery and fear-mongering. I even remember as a young child being warned by a well-meaning Sunday School teacher to stay away from the devil's activities going on at the Pentecostal church next door.

But the folks at my church seemed to embrace these gifts. They talked openly about them and taught classes on their activation and practice. They were not ashamed or secretive about the Holy Spirit. It was refreshing, and the pastor's encouragement of the expression of the gifts, under the leadership of the Holy Spirit, seemed a radical invitation for me to explore what I now felt I was missing.

As listed in 1 Corinthians 12, the nine gifts of the Spirit are:

Words of Wisdom
Words of Knowledge
Faith
Healing
Miraculous Powers
Prophesy
Distinguishing between spirits
Speaking in different kinds of tongues
 Interpretation of tongues

My goal here is not to explain each gift of the Spirit. (I refer you to the Resources appendix for that.) But it's important to understand that the gifts are an expression of the Holy Spirit himself. He releases them at his discretion to minister both through and to us. For example, in the moment that the Holy Spirit wanted to connect with me, he gave Lee the knowledge that I was in physical pain, gave him a dream about the blue tunnel, and showed him my just-finished painting. And Lee, highly-experienced in the practice of hearing and responding to the Holy Spirit, was the willing conduit through which the Holy Spirit began to minister to me.

In one situation the Holy Spirit may release words of knowledge, but in another situation the gift of supernatural healing is released. The point here is that the Holy Spirit himself is the activator, not us. When we open ourselves up to practice any of these gifts we are simply making ourselves available to hear and respond to what the Holy Spirit is doing.

As I began to explore and embrace the idea that I could actually experience any or all of these gifts as an expression of my growing relationship with the Holy Spirit, my story unfolded with greater clarity. I was wholeheartedly on board to experience them all - except maybe the spooky one about speaking in tongues. That one was just too weird for me!

But in my resolve to "test" each new experience through prayer and Scripture the gift of tongues has become to me the most endearing expression of the Holy Spirit.

JUST SING!

I popped a new *Jesus Culture Music*[47] disk into the car stereo as I headed out onto the highway. My forty-five minute commute to church had evolved into much-anticipated opportunities for personal worship - joyfully clocking the miles away with prayer, thanksgiving, and singing. On this particular Sunday morning, the current topic of the Prayer Tools class was on my mind: Praying in the Spirit.

I was learning that a prayer language was available to me as a benefit of my relationship with the Holy Spirit. But, because it was so closely related to the gift of tongues, I was hesitant to embrace it. Before the conclusion of each class, we were directed to break into small groups and pray together. Many expressed their prayers through their native English or Spanish, while others expressed themselves through their prayer language of tongues.

With my first exposure to it, I could feel anxiety rise in my spirit as I recalled the childhood warnings prohibiting the devil's work. But the experience of listening to these gentle expressions of unknown utterances was intoxicating. Each "language" was different - some consisted of short, staccato rhythms, while others flowed eloquently. Some bore the cadence of fully-formed languages; others seemed limited to words or phrases. Some just sounded like gibberish, but together the room hummed with a heavenly sound. It wasn't singing, but it was music just the same.

In chapter 14 of 1 Corinthians, the Apostle Paul talks a lot about the expression of the gift of tongues working in tandem with the gift of interpreting tongues in a public forum. He set forth guidelines for their practice so that believers and non-believer alike could be encouraged together. But he also talks about the grace of tongues, a personal prayer language, given to every Spirit-filled believer. Here's how Paul describes his own experience:

> *"For if I pray in a tongue, my spirit prays but my mind is unfruitful. What am I to do? I will pray with my spirit, but I will pray with my mind also; I will sing praise with my spirit, but I will also sing with my mind also."* (1 Corinthians 14:14, ESV)

So as I drove down the highway prayerfully considering and logically trying to figure out how my spirit could pray without my mind being involved, it dawned on me. If I would yield my mind, will and emotions to the Holy Spirit who lives in me, my spirit would be free to by-pass the filter of my brain and express itself freely. "But how do I do that, Lord?" I asked out loud. Unmistakably, I heard in my spirit:

Sing it out.

Just in that moment, the live-performance music on the CD shifted from vocal to instrumental as the vocalist encouraged the audience to "sing out in your own words." She herself began to sing in tongues, and what I was hearing on the CD sounded rather like scat singing. I was startled by that thought.

Think back to the jazz stylings of Frank Sinatra when he vocally improvised his now-famous "do-be-do-be-dos." That's scat singing. I'm not claiming that Sinatra's vocal improvisations were an expressing of a prayer language; but, without words, he was giving voice to the music he felt inside.

My analytical brain once again kicked into gear and was trying to make sense of a scat-singing prayer language when I was interrupted with commanding urgency:

Don't think. Just sing!

I opened my mouth in faith to scat sing and out came my prayer language! Within seconds I realized that I was no longer trying to scat sing, but syllables were being generated without my conceiving them first. I could stop and start at will and had no fear of being controlled or overwhelmed. It was a remarkably joyful experience, and I quickly became addicted to it.

I love to pray and sing in the Spirit. It encourages me, lifts me up, and releases me from carrying the burden of having to understand what my spirit *needs* to pray. I practice it in this way: I pray what's on my heart as far as my own words will take me, and then I yield my tongue to the Holy Spirit who takes over from there. The fact that I have no knowledge of the direction my prayer is taking under the leadership of the Holy Spirit is freeing. I focus my mind on the attributes of Jesus - how much he loves me and how he longs for me to become all he created me to be.

While praying in the Spirit I often receive the impression that I'm praying for someone or something specifically. Sometimes I'll receive the solution to a business problem or relationship struggle. Often I see in my mind's eye pictures or images that seem like video clips. When I pray from a place of fear, I receive peace. When my prayers feel weak, I become empowered. At other times I have absolutely no idea what I'm praying about. But what I do know is that the experience of spirit-to-Spirit communication is deeply intimate and faith-building. It releases in me a confidence to know that Jesus and the Holy Spirit are always interceding in prayerful agreement, and they've given me an open invitation to join in!

CHAPTER 11:

DISCOVERING ME

PALETTE OF POSSIBILITIES

With the release and practice of my prayer language came an increased sensitivity to things of the Spirit. The reading of Scripture seemed to take on a new dimension as passages that I had read for decades, memorized, and quoted often seemed to jump off the page with new insight. Scriptures that I could never quite comprehend before now had meaning. I was experiencing a spiritual awakening in the very core of my being. My spirit was soaring and, ironically, my intellect was struggling to keep pace.

As I became more and more comfortable with listening and responding to the promptings of the Holy Spirit, a funny phenomenon began to recur. I kept finding myself in the position of trying to "explain" to my brain what I was experiencing in my spirit. It was delightful evidence that Spirit-empowered wisdom and revelation was finally taking its rightful place above my ability to process through intellectual logic and reason. The pattern became: Respond to the promptings of the Holy Spirit first. Then ask for understanding later.

And such was the prayerful conversation I was having while working at my art table one afternoon. "Lord, how could I have read that Scripture for thirty years and not seen *that*?"

When I asked the question I wasn't really asking for an answer. I was simply standing at my art table cleaning my watercolor palette and celebrating how the Holy Spirit had brought the Scriptures to life with new meaning.

Your palette is the church.

That was a weird thought! I looked down at the paint palette before me. It was quite colorful, really. The newly-cleaned palette itself was shiny white, the center mixing area was empty and pristine, and I had just filled each paint compartment with freshly-squeezed paints from their tubes. To me it was the familiar 30 colors calling me to combine them into yet-to-be-seen artistic expressions. The possibilities were endless and the allure was intoxicating - always a moment to be enjoyed. Creativity was on the verge of being released.

"What does that have to do with church?" I pondered prayerfully.

With no response immediately forthcoming, I began the process of pulling select paints from their individual compartments out to the mixing area of the palette.

What are you doing?

It's just like the Holy Spirit to ask the obvious, so I responded matter-of-factly, "I'm painting."

What exactly are you doing?

"Exactly? I'm using water to release the paints. That way I can mix them together to get the color I want for the painting I have in mind to create. Why do you ask?"

I'm the water.

In that moment the Holy Spirit downloaded an explosion of understanding into my spirit. If the palette is the church, then the compartmentalized, straight-from-the-tube colors represent different denominational expressions. Perhaps one is Baptist, one is Anglican, and another is Pentecostal. When they stay confined to their place on the palette, they are simply pretty to look at. There on the palette they are limited to great potential. It is only through the power of the Holy Spirit, the "releasing" agent, that their *potential* will be brought together to fulfill the creative expression that God has in mind for Jesus' bride, the church.

In the same way, individual Scriptures may remain only partially understood, compartmentalized, until the Holy Spirit releases their full potential. As any concentrate requires a releasing agent, like water, to convert it into a usable solvent, so the Bible often remains in concentrated form until we allow the Holy Spirit to release its potential for Spirit-empowered living.

But, wait! There's more!! The power of the Holy Spirit as a releasing agent is not limited to the church and to the Scriptures. The Holy Spirit is poised to activate us, as well.

> *"For we are his (God's) workmanship, created in Christ Jesus for good works, which God prepared beforehand, that we should walk in them."*
> (Ephesians 2:10, ESV)

I sat there in front of my palette never before having considered God as the painter of me. Did he use a palette? Perhaps the compartmentalized colors on his palette represent my personality traits, talents or DNA. Perhaps they are the varied experiences of my life, both those in the past and those yet to come. Perhaps they are simply the supernatural elements of God's creativity.

As I try to articulate what my spirit came to understand that day, words fail me. But I can tell you that a sense of awe washed over me as I considered God's painting of me. He set up the palette and had all the creative elements lined up. But, oddly, enough, he included me in the creative process. When I responded to the Holy Spirit's prompting to receive Jesus as my savior, I "see" God moving my compartmentalized colors onto the cleaned palette. My old nature was replaced with my new nature in Jesus.

Decades later when I discovered the ministry of the Holy Spirit and began to yield to his promptings in my life, the colors in the mixing area came alive with creative possibilities. When the Holy Spirit, as the releasing agent, began to mix the colors of me, I was poised to become all God created me to be - to explore *"the riches of his (Jesus') glorious inheritance in the saints, and his incomparably great power for us who believe."*[48] Paradoxically, the resulting "painting" is not a picture of me, at all. It's a developing picture of who Jesus is - his nature and loving attributes being expressed through me.

"*In the beginning, God created . . .*"[49] From the first brush strokes of God's creativity he has been extending an invitation for his creations to join him in expressing his nature. He is a loving Father who longs to restore the hearts of his sons and daughters. He is calling us, Spirit-to-spirit, into a place of intimacy with him where he can activate and release in us all he designed us to be.

LET'S PAINT!

It was the afternoon of my friend Jennifer's birthday, and I was looking forward to the evening's celebration with her and Sherrie. Weeks earlier I had asked Jennifer what she would like for her birthday. She didn't hesitate for a moment, but replied enthusiastically, "I'd love one of your paintings!" Relieved that shopping would not be involved, I readily agreed to the project. My tight schedule at that time prohibited me from tackling a new painting before her birthday, but she gracefully received my promise of a forthcoming, belated gift.

With about an hour to spare before I needed to leave, I sat down with Jennifer's birthday card in hand, intending to write her a note of encouragement. Prayerfully, I asked, "Lord, what would you like me to write?"

Instantaneously, I heard in my spirit:

Let's paint her a picture!

I was startled by the childlike enthusiasm of the Holy Spirit's suggestion, like a little girl's uninhibited declaration, "Mommy, let's twirl!" It was full of life, energy, and joy. But with only an hour to spare, I reminded the Holy Spirit of both my time limitation and Jennifer's willingness to wait for a belated painting.

Let's paint! Come on. It'll be fun!!

Because my primary paint medium at the time was watercolor and my typical painting styles were portraiture and photo realism, hours of pre-planning were required before the brush ever hit the paper. I tried to explain this to the Holy Spirit, "Of course, it's fun, but I don't have time. Could we please focus on Jen's card so I can leave on time. What should I write?"

No writing. Let's paint!!!

After several minutes of trying to shake it off I finally relented and headed to my art table. I confess, however, that my obedience was tainted with mutterings about "not enough time" and "being late." Hurriedly, I prepared a small piece of watercolor paper and opened my palette, all the while thinking dismissively, "I don't have time for this."

As I predicted in my not-enough-time mindset, the painting was a disaster. In my hurried approach, I had haphazardly laid the colors in too fast and ended up with a muddy mess. "Lord, there's not enough time to do this right. It looks like a three-year-old painted this. Why do I have to do this right now? . . ."

My spew of frustrated rhetoric was interrupted by the Holy Spirit's patient prompting:

Are you done, yet?

"Yes, Lord." I waited.

Take out another piece of paper and, this time? – let's do it together.

I quieted my spirit before the blank piece of paper and listened. What followed was a remarkable experience of interactive creative expression as the Holy Spirit prompted me. It felt like a master painter was standing next to me, encouraging and directing every brush stroke. Here's an abbreviated version of the promptings:

Let's start with a soft background of warm colors. Pick whichever ones you like.

OK. That's good. Wait. Save some of the white space for later.

I like pink! Put a little more pink there. Make it darker. That's it.

Do you have any gouache? White?

Great! Put a dot of white gouache right there. I like that. Now, two more dots - up a little more. There! Yes, right there.

What do you see here? Do that.

Cool! I like what you just did. Do more of that. OK, stop. That's perfect.

Now, take your brush and gently smudge those white dots. Wispy, with an upward stroke. That's enough.

Look at how the color is drying over here. I love that!!

Tilt the paper just a bit to make the color run. Now just a bit the other direction. Lovely!

OK. That's it. We're done. Jen's going to love it!!

Twenty minutes had passed as I took direction from the Holy Spirit and laid onto paper a creative expression of supernatural origin. In reverent awe, I examined the painting. The colors were clear and bright. It was fresh and pure and full of life. Abstract in nature, this petite painting was mesmerizing to me. I pulled out my first attempt and set the two paintings side by side. No comparison.

See what we can do when we partner together!

I laughed.

Better get going or you'll be late!

I looked at my watch and chuckled that I had five minutes to spare before my originally-scheduled departure time. I quickly ran a hair-dryer over the painting to set the colors, grabbed my purse and keys, secured the dogs and headed toward the car. As I turned to lock the back door, I heard the Holy Spirit "taunt" me with good-natured enthusiasm:

See? I told you it would be fun!

IN JOY!

WHAT DOVE?

Needless to say, my drive across town that evening was full of joyful praise. What an amazing experience that was! I couldn't understand it, but that didn't seem to matter. The Holy Spirit had awakened something deep in my spiritual core and time would eventually reveal its full impact.

Ironically, I arrived early and took a minute to write on the back of the painting some encouraging words that I felt the Holy Spirit wanted me to say to Jennifer. And, not surprisingly, he arranged time for me to share both my painting experience and the painting itself with her before Sherrie joined us. True to her nature, Jennifer celebrated with enthusiasm the painting, the painter, and the ultimate Creator.

"I love the dove!" She said as she examined the painting at arm's length.

"What dove?" I asked.

"Right there." She pointed.

Remember the three dots of white gouache and the direction for wispy brush strokes? Sure enough, those dots had morphed into the image of a dove without me even realizing it. Another wave of awe crashed over me. How could I have painted that? No planning. No expectation. Only the prompting of the Holy Spirit. It was humbling. It was uplifting. It was perfectly delightful.

When Sherrie arrived at the birthday celebration, Jennifer and I showed her the painting, and I retold my painting experience. She, too, saw the dove, but also found other insights within the painting: freedom, a woman's facial profile, spiritual rebirth. "This is a picture of life in the Spirit." she said animatedly. "God is releasing his prophetic voice through your paintings. I think there will be many more to come."

That petite painting, *Life in the Spirit*, now framed and hanging in Jennifer's living room, was, indeed, the first of many. Occasionally, Jennifer tells me of a new visitor to her home who received a completely different insight in and through that painting. How cool is that? The Holy Spirit directed the creation of a painting through which he would continue to speak - each interpretation being uniquely oriented to the person he brings to view it.

And so a new chapter of my life began in the wake of Jehovah Sneaky's mischievous and delightful introduction into the world of "prophetic" painting.

EXPLORING PROPHESY

Prophesy is an Old Testament thing, right? Jeremiah and Isaiah declaring destruction and judgment because of Israel's rebelliousness. Samuel's chastisements against idol worship and warnings of calamity. Amos and Obadiah proclaiming plunder and destruction as a consequence of prideful disobedience. Daniel and Ezekiel describing unimaginable creatures and mysterious future events. Even John the Baptist, who appears in the New Testament, joins them with his urgent plea to *"Repent! For the kingdom of heaven is at hand."*[50]

Having grown up under the demonic oppression of a debilitating fear of fire, Old Testament prophesies were something I tried to avoid. I wanted nothing to do with all that talk of fire, destruction, and calamity! As a scared, eight-year-old I trusted in Jesus to protect me from my impending, fiery doom. I knew from that decisive moment forward that my salvation was assured. I had no doubt that I would spend eternity in heaven and escape the fires of hell. But, unknowingly, I allowed Satan to use God's Word as an instrument to perpetuate my fear - a reminder to watch my "Ps and Qs" lest God strike me down with fire and calamity. Fear became the primary motivation for five decades of my performance-based Christianity!

But once free from that fear-based oppression, assured of God's unfailing love for me, and growing in my ability to hear God's voice, I wanted to explore the Holy Spirit's gift of prophesy. After all, my hesitancy to embrace the gift of tongues had emerged into a beautiful expression of personal intimacy with God through the Holy Spirit. Maybe prophesy would prove fruitful, as well.

I wanted to reconcile the gloom-and-doom prophetic voices of the Old Testament with the enthusiastic and child-like promptings of the Holy Spirit who had directed me through my first prophetic painting. This dichotomy didn't make sense to me, so I began to explore what the New Testament gift of prophesy might look like when exercised in the modern world.

I came to understand that the people of Israel in the Old Testament lived in a "visitational" culture. God would "rest" his presence for a period of time and then lift back off. Obedience and humility attracted his Presence. Rebellion, idolatry and disobedience caused his Presence to retreat. The Old Testament prophets, however, seemed to carry the wisdom and revelation of God as their lifestyle. They were the voice of God to their entire generation. Kings and leaders would seek God's wisdom through the prophets because, at that time, only a prophet could hear God's voice.

When sin entered in through Adam and Eve, God could not allow His holiness to be tainted by their fallen state. If he had, mankind would have been lost forever. As evidenced in the stories of the Old Testament, mankind could not accomplish their own restoration. They, and we, were doomed for destruction.

Then Jesus stepped into history to usher in a Kingdom-based, "habitational" culture. He came to reconnect us to God. Through the finished work of the cross, Jesus took onto himself all of God's wrath for every sin, every rebellion, every disobedient act ever committed for all past and future generations. He paid the price so we don't have to. Please understand: I did not accept Jesus as my Savior and then wait for him to pay the price for my sinfulness. He had already paid it in full. He had already taken on God's righteous anger for my sin, paid my penalty, and set me free from condemnation. I simply chose to receive the benefits of what Jesus had already done for me.

With all of his anger poured out on Jesus, God has no anger left for us. We are *"new creations in Christ Jesus."*[51] As believers, our regenerated hearts are now able to host the very presence of God - to "habitate" with God's Holy Spirit. Did you know that King David, in one of his psalms, describes us?

> *"But you, Lord, sit enthroned forever;*
> *your renown endures through all generations. . . .*
> *Let this be written for a **future** generation,*
> *that **a people not yet created** may praise the Lord."*
> (Psalm 102:12;18, NIV)

We are the *"people not yet created!"* How fantastic is that? We are *"new creations in Christ,"* living with God's Holy Spirit inside of us. Think about the significance of that for a moment. Never before had mankind been able to host the Presence of God in their human hearts. But Jesus' finished work on the cross made it possible for us to receive a new heart – literally.

This supernatural exchange means we get to hear His voice, to follow Jesus' example of living in right relationship with God through the indwelling power of the Holy Spirit. We get to walk in the promise of Jesus:

> *"Truly, truly, I say to you, whoever believes in me will also do the works that I do; and greater works than these will he do, because I am going to the Father. Whatever you ask in my name, this I will do, that the Father may be glorified in the Son. If you ask me anything in my name, I will do it."* (John 14:12-14, ESV)

Jesus was the first of the New Testament prophets. Even before the cross, his words began to change the culture, *"You have heard it said, but I say . . ."*[52] He was ushering in a paradigm shift of the heart - old covenant out; new covenant on the immediate horizon. The new covenant would be sealed by his coming death and resurrection, and new words would be needed to describe this forth-coming reality. Jesus spoke of unconditional love, freedom from oppression and condemnation, glorious revelations yet to be experienced, new facets of our identities that are ours to explore, peace that surpasses understanding, and abounding joy. Better still, Jesus promised that his words would be available to us through the indwelling Holy Spirit:

> *"When the Spirit of truth comes, he will guide you into all the truth, for he will not speak on his own authority, but whatever he hears he will speak, and he will declare to you the things that are to come. He will glorify me, for he will take what is mine and declare it to you."* (John 16: 13, ESV)

This is the Spirit behind the modern-day expression of the gift of prophesy. Jesus makes the things of God known to the Holy Spirit living in us. The Holy Spirit, in turn, reveals it to us. When we position ourselves to hear and respond in obedience, we receive the privilege of releasing words of encouragement and comfort both to ourselves and to the people around us, both believers and non-believers alike.

CHAPTER 12:

PAINTING HIS VOICE

IT'S GONNA BE FUN!

It was a typical Sunday morning except for the traffic. Construction on US Highway 114 had detoured traffic and, although the traffic was light, reducing everyone down to one exit lane had brought us all to a crawl. "Finally!" I thought as I pulled into the church parking lot and hastily made my way inside.

I was doing my power-walking best to make it to class on time when my focused determination was thwarted by a glance into another classroom. I caught a glimpse of an artist's easel, canvas, drop cloth, and paints just as the classroom door was being closed. Curiosity got the better of me. Forgetting my original destination, I slipped into the back of the room to satisfy it.

The artist, Anne, introduced herself and taught about expressing the impressions of the Holy Spirit onto canvas. I drank it all in. During the activation portion, she invited class members to listen to the Holy Spirit and then come "finger" paint their impressions. Although this was not a classroom full of artists, there was little hesitancy as one after another added their creative marks. The Holy Spirit was stirring in me as I watched the creativity unfold before me. The resulting painting, coupled with the spoken expressions of what the Holy Spirit had impressed upon each participant, left an unmistakable impression on me.

At the conclusion of the class I sought a private audience with Anne and introduced myself. Then, gesturing with my hand toward the canvas and easel in a circular motion, I said, "I'm not exactly sure what all *this* is about, but I feel strongly that I'm supposed to be a part of it." Without hesitation she invited me to join her and the other prophetic artists on the following Monday night at one of our satellite campuses. As I left that classroom pondering the phrase "prophetic artist," I felt like the Holy Spirit was jumping around inside of me declaring like a enthusiastic cheerleader:

Fun. Fun. FUN!! This is gonna be fun!! Aren't you excited? We're going to have so much fun! I can't wait.

I didn't hesitate to align my spirit with the Holy Spirit's enthusiastic promptings. I was excited, too. Something deep in my creative spirit was being called forth, and I felt it bubbling up to the surface. I couldn't identify or explain what I was feeling; but, with uncharacteristic enthusiasm, I couldn't wait for Monday night to roll around.

As I soon discovered, the activities of the prophetic painting team occurred under the umbrella of the church's Healing Ministry. Monday nights were set aside with an open invitation. Anyone who had a need for physical healing could come and receive prayer. I found it to be an uplifting atmosphere. It was purposefully designed as a setting for prayer, contemplation, and worship. Those who came for prayer were encouraged to rest and "soak" in the Presence of God while awaiting their turn with the prayer team volunteers. The prophetic artists contributed to the "soaking" atmosphere by offering an alternative focus. Why concentrate on pain and fear when God is creating and releasing something new before your very eyes?

I felt quite at home during my inaugural visit to this setting. Anne greeted me warmly and encouraged, "Take some time to listen to what the Holy Spirit is saying and then simply paint what He releases. Feel free to engage the people around you. Talk to them about what you are painting or what God is saying to you. Have fun with it. We finish up around 8:30 and you may keep your painting or give it away." And with that launch I stepped into my destiny.

PAINTING HIS VOICE

Many of you, I'm sure, have seen the movie "Chariots of Fire." As the recipient of the Oscar Award for Best Picture in 1982, it's based on the true-life experiences of Scottish runner Eric Lidell and his quest to compete for gold at the 1924 Olympic games in Paris. I was in my mid-twenties when the movie was released, and one scene in that movie has stayed with me to this day. It's the poignant moment when Eric reveals to his sister why he must continue his pursuit to compete in the games against conflicting callings, staggering odds and opposing advice:

> "I believe God made me for a purpose, but he also made me fast. And when I run, I feel His pleasure."[53]

Feeling unlovable and crippled by fear, I sat in that movie theater as a young woman and wondered enviously what it must feel like to know the purpose God created you to fulfill and to feel God's pleasure when doing it. What freedom there must be in that! It was a pipe dream, at best, to my youthful heart.

My physical healing thirty years later was a turning point for me. Of course, it was significant to my physical well-being in the natural. But, even more so, it was the catalyst for the awakening of my Jesus-centered, spiritual well-being. Through the pathway of healing came abiding and worship, followed by freedom and a deepening of my personal intimacy with God. As I made myself available to the ministry of the Holy Spirit, he began to call out and release my true identity.

God designed Eric Lidell to run fast. God designed me to paint his voice.

It's no longer about what I want to paint. It's about what God wants to paint through me. I position myself before the canvas and listen with my spirit. Then, by faith, I begin to paint what I hear him say. It's an incredibly intimate experience that inspires in me both awe and wonder. The God who created the heavens and the earth whispers creativity into *my* ear, and I get to release it onto canvas. How fun is that?!

But, far more significantly, it's not about me, at all. And it's not about the painting, either. It's about what God wants to say through the painting to someone specific. My experience with prophetic painting has taught me that God *always* speaks through each painting and, more often than not, he speaks directly to an intended viewer with an intentional message. My job is to listen, paint, and facilitate that connection as the Holy Spirit leads me.

PUZZLING PUZZLE

So, as Monday afternoon came to a close, I loaded my art supplies into the trunk of my car and reminded God again that I didn't have his answer. Dallas rush-hour traffic gave way to Irving rush-hour gridlock as I sat in a standstill on Interstate-183 trying to head west.

"Where am I going, Lord?" I asked, *again*.

God and I had been having this on-going, one-sided conversation for a week, now. I had two events I wanted to attend that Monday night, and I simply couldn't decide on either. Both were spiritually significant, but I couldn't be in two places at the same time. I had decided to leave the outcome to God's direction. But, so far, he wasn't talking much on the subject.

I reminded him again, "The Loop 360 exit is about 12 miles ahead, Lord. Should I take it to the prayer meeting or do you want me to paint tonight at the Healing Rooms?" I positioned myself in the middle lane to respond to either answer. Another mile or two passed slowly in silence.

"You just let me know, Lord, when you're ready." I chuckled to myself and began to worship out loud in my prayer language as I continued my crawl-paced approach toward the Loop 360 exit. Then, suddenly, I surprised myself when my prayer language was interrupted with a startling exclamation in English, "Lord, I love how you fit the puzzle pieces together!" Immediately, I began to process my seemingly random declaration.

"Lord, I *do* love how you make connections, but what are you trying to say to me?" In my mind's eye I began to see an image of puzzle pieces coming together. Although I didn't understand the exact meaning, thoughts of all the puzzle pieces God had connected in my life gave rise to more worship. In the midst of all this delightful distraction, I suddenly realized that I had completely missed my Loop 360 exit! Another wave of delight washed over me, knowing that, tonight, I was supposed to go to the Healing Rooms and paint puzzle pieces!

Let me just say that the painting process that night was a bizarre struggle. The Holy Spirit and I had artistic differences. The puzzle image I had in mind, was not what he had in mind. The dialogue in my spirit played out something like this:

"Shouldn't the puzzle pieces line up?" I inquired prayerfully.

Nope. I like it like that.

The painting process continued as I questioned every direction I heard. "This is awful, Lord. I don't like these colors, at all!"

I do!

The colors were clashing and there seemed to be no artistic composition at all. Every few minutes I nagged, "Shouldn't we just start over?"

Nope. Keep painting.

I could not make sense of this painting. It was embarrassing to me. Not my style. Not my colors. Not what I had in mind, at all! And, bizarrely enough, no one around me stopped to talk or inquire about what God was saying through the painting. I prayerfully complained some more. "See, Lord, no one else likes it either!"

It's not for them.

I continued to paint with a grumbling spirit, "Well, I hope it's not for me, because I don't like it."

I know. Keep painting.

The image on the canvas became even more unsightly as I felt directed to add chaotic dots and rays of white paint all over it. It was a mess!

When I finally felt that this bewildering image was complete, I left it displayed on the easel against my rising desire to hide it away all together. I walked away to distance myself from it and watched as it seemed everyone was avoiding it. I closed my eyes and earnestly sought an answer in prayer, "Lord, what was that all about?" The Holy Spirit reminded me again that prophetic painting was not about me. Obedience was what he desired of me. I asked him to forgive my impertinence as I felt His prompting.

Do you trust me?

I opened my eyes to see a young woman standing in front of the painting with her back to me. She stood there for a long time. "Lord, what does she see in that painting?"

Go ask her.

I approached and, touching her on the shoulder so as not to startle her from behind, gently said, "I'm the artist of this painting, and I'd love to know what God is speaking to you through it." She turned toward me with tears on her cheek and said, "God just answered my prayer."

I did not know how to interpret her tears. They seemed sad and joyful, both at the same time. She began to tell me the story of how she came to the Healing Rooms to stand in for her teenage brother who suffers the victimization of autism. "I was drawn to the puzzle pieces in the painting because puzzle pieces are the symbol of the National Autism Society. But as I looked more closely at the painting, I realized that God was answering my prayer."

She told of her frustration at not being able to understand her brother's experience and how she had asked the Lord to show her what goes on in his mind. "You painted it!" she said, her voice seemingly in awe that God had answered her prayer but yet disturbed by the turbulence of the image itself. Sadness was in her voice when she said introspectively, "It's so chaotic in there."

Quite to my surprise I responded enthusiastically, "God's not finished, yet."

She looked up at me with a perplexed expression on her face as I began to tell her what I felt the Holy Spirit wanted to say through the painting. The interpretation came out so clearly that I, too, was a bit surprised by it.

"This painting may show you the chaos of your brother's mind, but God isn't finished, yet. We, as humans, take a puzzle from its box, pour it out on the table, and what's the first thing we do? We look for all the edge pieces first. Once we have the border of the picture complete, we begin to fill in the picture according the known image on the box cover. Right?"

She shook her head in agreement.

"God doesn't work like that. He works from the inside out." I pointed to the painting, "These puzzle pieces here in the middle are not lined up, but they're coming together. The rays of white are the creative bursts of energy God is using to bring the pieces into alignment. They are your prayers. Can you see it? God is using the power of your prayers, and those of your family, to continue the healing process in your brother. Have you seen any improvement in him, lately?"

"Yes," she said as her face lit up a bit, "He's been getting better the last nine months. That's why I came here - to have y'all pray for him again!"

Redirecting her back to the painting, the Holy Spirit gave me the words to say: "See all these white dots out here in the outer area? Those are the prayers that you've yet to pray. And when you do pray them, God will give them power as he begins to move all the puzzle pieces that are along the edge. See? The ones that seem to be falling off the edge of the canvas? God will bring them all into his alignment in his timing. Trust that he is doing a healing work in your brother's mind and spirit. Keep praying. God knows what the finished puzzle looks like. Wait confidently for him to reveal it to you."

I prayed a simple prayer of blessing and sent the painting home with her as a reminder of the encouragement the Holy Spirit had just released to her. And from that amazing experience forward, I have never again questioned what the Holy Spirit asks me to paint.

Sometimes he interprets a prophetic painting directly to the intended recipient. Other times, like with the puzzle painting, he gives me the interpretation to speak out. Sometimes the paintings convict. Sometimes they direct. But most often, the paintings encourage people to see God in a new way, allowing them to be touched unexpectedly by the power of God's creative energy as he speaks to them on a very personal level. And I've seen that Jesus loves to release physical and emotional healing through these divinely-creative encounters.

I love prophetic painting! I was made to paint God's voice. When I get to do that in the context of encouragement, healing prayers and prophetic words, I know that I am living out what God designed me to do! Like Eric Lidell discovered, I, too, have discovered that God made *me* for a purpose. He made me to paint his voice. And in the intimacy of that creative process, I feel his pleasure.

PAINTING HIS VOICE

CHAPTER 13:

CALL TO DREAM

TIME TO DREAM

As I begin to bring the telling of my story to a close, the Holy Spirit is reminding me that my story has plenty of chapters yet to be written. My future contains many more paintings to be painted, more people to encourage, and more spiritual battles to win. The chronic, debilitating fear that once made me dread my future has been rendered powerless by the discovery of my true identify in Jesus. Religious duty and ritual obligation have given way to the freedom of exploring true intimacy with my Creator. The Holy Spirit has released me from earth-bound thinking and is calling me to dream his dreams and share *his* story.

EVELINE

Eveline and I first crossed paths on moving day when I helped my parents move into their retirement community two years ago. Eveline lives in the next-door apartment, and I have loved her from the moment I met her. She feels the same way about me. Now in her mid-nineties and exhibiting moments of diminishing mental capacity, she still carries herself with the grace and dignity that I imagine she exhibited in her youth. Her spirit is refreshingly pure and gentle.

I leaned down to hug her as she sat in the lobby waiting for her son to arrive. It was Mother's Day, and she was dressed in fine style. I sat down to visit with her, and in a moment of uncharacteristic mental clarity she asked, "Why do I love you so much?" I replied with an affectionate response, but she was earnestly seeking a tangible answer. "We've loved each from the moment we met, and I've never done that with anyone before. Why do you think that is?"

This was not casual banter. She earnestly wanted to know. I answered, "I think Jesus *in you* loves Jesus *in me*. That's why we're drawn to each other."

We had never had a discussion of spiritual things before. "Yes, maybe that's it," she said gently. We sat in silence for a moment as I sensed she was processing her thoughts. "No. There's something more. There's something about you that's different."

I felt the nudge of the Holy Spirit and responded. "Eveline, I believe what you're sensing in me is the Holy Spirit."

She quickly made eye contact and perked up her expression, "Do you know the Holy Spirit? Personally? You *know* Him?"

Before I could respond she looked away toward the window and began what seemed like a ramble-in-the-making, "There was a little Baptist Church in East Texas way back . . . " I thought her moments of lucid thought had just slipped away when I realized that her story was still on point. She told of attending this small church as a young woman when a circuit preacher came to town. "He told us about the Holy Spirit." she explained to me.

"What did he say?" I asked as I could feel her emotions shifting and tears began to form in her eyes.

"I don't remember." She said, "But what he said made me cry. I wasn't sad or upset. It's just that something came over me, and I started to cry. I couldn't stop. I cried all day long." She looked at me to gauge my reaction as she continued, "I was so ashamed. I couldn't stop crying, and my friends told me I needed to see a counselor or a doctor. Everyone was worried about me because I couldn't tell them why I was crying. They said I was having a nervous breakdown."

My heart went out to her with such compassion, "No, sweetheart," I assured her vulnerable heart, "You weren't having a nervous breakdown. You were having an encounter with the Holy Spirit."

"I was?" she brightened up. "Will you tell me about the Holy Spirit?"

We had a wonderful conversation as I told her about a similar can't-stop-crying encounter that I had had with the Holy Spirit. "Really?" She responded with delight in her eyes as she continued, "I thought I was crazy! All those years ago and I've never forgotten that day."

She giggled with such glee as we hugged, and I felt freedom wash over her. She pulled back to look me in the eyes. "I just knew that someday someone would come to tell me more about the Holy Spirit. *Now* I know why I love you so much!"

I think back on that Mother's Day with bittersweet emotion. My joy of seeing Eveline receive healing in her spirit was tainted by the thought of all the years she spent feeling ashamed and confused about her supernatural encounter with the Holy Spirit. The people around her had no frame of reference and their dismissive comments were not meant to be hurtful. They had simply spoken out of their lack of experience and understanding.

DREAMING GOD'S DREAMS

Oh, how my heart longs for everyone to experience the freedom of walking out their God-ordained destiny with joy and confidence - to unplug from the constraints of religion, humanism, self-actualization, and secularism. None of that matters in light of who God really is and who he created each of us to become. It's a journey of exploration. The Holy Spirit is our guide, and Jesus is our assurance.

I believe we are living in the time of the fulfillment of the Prophet Joel's declaration:

"I will pour out my Spirit on all people.
Your sons and daughters will prophesy,
your old men will dream dreams,
your young men will see visions,
Even on my servants, both men and women,
I will pour out my Spirit in those days." (Joel 2:28-29, NIV)

We are living in *"those days!"* The Holy Spirit is poised and ready to initiate the awakening of our spirits. We are the *"people not yet created,"*[54] and Jesus has made a way to purify our hearts so we can carry the very Presence of God within us. We are God's individual masterpieces of unique craftsmanship. He designed us each with a purpose, and the outpouring of the Holy Spirit will guide us into our true identities, fully-resourced with power, purpose and confidence.

As people on the earth today, I believe we are living in the infancy of this season of outpouring. We are uniquely positioned to see and do our part in the unveiling of God's ultimate plan. It will be awesome. It will be powerful. It will be undeniable. And I'm confident that it will be supernaturally creative - unlike anything the world has experienced before:

"No eye has seen, no ear has heard, no heart has imagined, what God has prepared for those who love him." (1 Corinthians 2:9, Berean)

I take that as a promise from God himself, and I definitely want to be part of that! I feel him calling me to champion a new vision - His vision: To participate in creating a unique house of God - an environment. An empowering atmosphere dedicated to the creative expressions of the Holy Spirit. A creative atmosphere where the experience of worship ushers in and releases the prophetic arts. A place where prayer dancers can dance, prophetic artists can paint or sculpt, musicians can create or record, and authors can write. Space available for individual, creativity studios. Galleries for permanent and rotating art exhibitions. Rooms set aside for creative teaching, prayer, deliverance and healing. Coffee bar and gathering spaces. A resource center for the purchase of faith-based books, music, and art. Events that encourage worship and the prophetic expressions of the Holy Spirit, declaring to God's children who they really are and who they can become in Christ. A place of sanctuary from the oppressiveness of the world's negativity. A place where hope and optimism abound. A place where the Holy Spirit is free to be himself and we are free to explore all he has for us!

My heart races at the thought that my journey could contribute to the creation of such an amazing place. That's my dream.

And this is my prayer: That you, too, would discover your true identity in Christ, live out your God-ordained purpose, and feel his pleasure wash over you. It's a journey of delightful discovery, and I highly recommend it!

You may be at the beginning of your journey as you feel the Holy Spirit tugging at your heart and inviting you to take that first step of faith - to let Jesus wash away your past and step into the freedom he has waiting for you. You may be a new believer in Jesus, exploring what it looks like to walk out your new-found faith. Perhaps you love the Lord with all your heart, but the lies of Satan feel stronger than the truth of who Jesus *really* is. Are you patiently and dutifully *"bearing your cross unto death"*[55]? Maybe you're a church-going believer bound by tradition and religious obligation, not even knowing that a whole new dimension of Spirit-filled empowerment is available to you. Perhaps God has sent an interesting character into your life, like Lee, to challenge what you *think you know* about who God is. And maybe – hopefully - you've said "yes" to the Holy Spirit as he invites you, even right now, to join him in the journey of discovering your true identity and walking out your God-inspired purpose.

There are many other "maybe" statements that might define you, but these are mine. They describe my journey. And my prayer for you is that something about my spiritual journey will resonate with you. That through it you may be inspired to make yourself available to the call on your life - to become all God created you to be, to explore Spirit-empowered possibilities, and to live captivated by the overwhelming love Jesus has for you. Come and join me! It's never too late to begin walking in joy as your Creator is inviting you to join him in the unveiling of his uniquely-designed purpose for your life.

CALL TO DREAM

CHAPTER 14:

YOU ARE TREASURE!

YOU ARE TREASURE!

I thought I was finished telling my story, but I feel the Holy Spirit prompting me to share a parting thought. It's a story - a parable from the book of Matthew:

> *"The kingdom of heaven is like treasure hidden in a field. When a man found it, he hid it again, and then in his joy went and sold all he had and bought that field.* (Matthew 13:45, NIV)

> *"Again, the kingdom of heaven is like a merchant looking for fine pearls. When he found one of great value, he went away and sold everything he had and bought it."* (Matthew 13:44-46, NIV)

The interpretation of this parable is simple: The man in the story is Jesus, the field is the world, and you are the "hidden" treasure. *You* are the pearl of great value!

Jesus designed you from before the beginning of time. He "hid" you for a season - perhaps while you were yet unborn; perhaps while you were still held back by sin or unbelief. But Jesus knows you by name. He knows your true value. After all, he created you!

And while you were still "hidden," Jesus went away to secure his ownership of you. You were too great a treasure, too beautiful a pearl, for him to leave you "hidden." He could not bear the possibility that you could be lost to another's bid for your affection. So Jesus went and paid the highest price - up front, as is, no questions asked, no returns allowed. He bought you with his life.

Jesus was thinking only of you, his pearl of great value, when he voluntarily took the punishment for all of your sins - past, present, and future. Because a righteous and holy God must deal with sin, God poured out his divine anger on Jesus so that he would not have to pour it out on you. That's the good news of the cross! The price has been paid and Jesus' resurrection sealed the deal.

But why would Jesus choose to do that for you - for you, specifically?

Because he knew from the beginning who he created you to become. And he knew you could never step into your divine purpose with the burden of death and the astronomical debt of sin weighing you down. In his joy, knowing your amazing value, Jesus paid the price willingly.[56] And he did it with no strings attached. Seriously! He did it before you were born. He didn't wait for you to sin to see how bad a penalty he would have to pay. He paid it all, and he did it without you. But he did it *for* you.

You have divine value. You are the pearl of great value. You were purchased at an exorbitant price. You are treasure! And when you accept by faith what Jesus' overwhelming love has done for you, he can begin the process of removing you from your place of "hidden-ness."

But what does a Savior do with a dirty pearl?

He begins to wipe away your encumbering dirt, exposing your underlying beauty. He speaks life over you, reminding you how beautiful you are and how you are so worth the price he chose to pay for you. Then he invites the Holy Spirit to begin the process of polishing you - his freshly-cleaned, deeply-loved pearl of great value. Together, they lovingly expose you to the Jeweler's light, enhancing your rare and beautiful qualities.

And here's the best part (as if the news wasn't already great enough): Like a diamond being placed securely within the prongs of a ring or a pearl within a necklace, God has prepared a setting just for you. And since only you can fill it, Jesus and the Holy Spirit are committed to helping you become all you were created to be - to show you the brilliance with which they can shine through you!

YOU ARE TREASURE!

IMPASSIONED STORIES

POWER IN THE PAINTINGS!

It is such a privilege to partner with the Holy Spirit in creating paintings that have impact and allow people to connect directly to the heart of God – to hear his voice and connect with him in unexpected and supernatural ways.

I pray you'll enjoy reading these stories as much as I love telling them. For in them are contained the very essence of a supernatural Father who loves to release heaven into the earth through creative expression and empowering encounters.

For confidentiality purposes I have changed the names of those whose stories I'm about to share. But, be assured, their heavenly Father knows them intimately and rejoices over each and every one.

IN JOY!

"LIFE IN THE SPIRIT"

These are the paintings I described in Chapter 10 as I recalled my introduction to the world of prophetic painting. Honestly, I would rather you not see the first painting - it doesn't reflect well on my artistic abilities, and I have a strong desire to run it through a shredder!

But I humbly present it here, not only as a personal, character-building exercise, but also to show you how impactful the Holy Spirit's guidance is on the creation of my paintings. The contrast is undeniable.

As I look at these two images placed so closely in proximity to one another, I sense that the Holy Spirit is prompting me to recognize something anew: These images represent a painted metaphor of my life - before and after I discovered Spirit-empowered living. The contrast could not be more dramatic! And I could not be more thankful!

IMPASSIONED STORIES

"THE ELEVENTH HOUR"

As I asked the question, "Holy Spirit, what do you want to paint tonight?" the canvas loomed intimidating large before me. It had been donated and was much larger than I was used to. I waited prayerfully for direction:

Start with blue.

As I stood before the canvas with a palette full of blue in my hand, I closed my eyes to focus and wait on further direction. Immediately, in my mind's eye, I saw and felt waves of encircling blue.

It took the full extension of my arm to sweep the blue onto this large canvas and the experience was freeing. As the first "waves" began to take shape, the lead pastor of the healing team stopped by with a fun testimony.

"I was outside just now praying and walking around the perimeter of the building," he said with a touch of excitement in his voice as he continued. "I saw the Holy Spirit encircling the building with his Presence, and it was blue. Then I walked in and immediately saw you painting the same thing!"

The confirmation was invigorating, and I got lost in the fun of creating these Holy Spirit waves. Throughout the experience, I kept asking in my spirit, "What is this, Lord?" Most often I sense that it's the Holy Spirit's voice I hear in response to my questions, but on this evening it felt like Jesus answered:

I'm disclosing myself in the fullness of time.

Honestly, that made no sense to me, but I continued to seek understanding as the blue waves on the canvas began to form a portal. I felt compelled to add accents of red and orange, followed by wispy vertical strokes of white. I stepped back, thinking the painting was finished but did not yet feel settled in my spirit. Without any forethought at all, I boldly stepped up to the canvas and quickly placed a series of small vertical strokes at the portal's edge. Now it felt complete.

As I stepped back to view the painting, I realized that a gathering of folks was behind me. I love to ask the question, "What do you see?" And to this question that night there was no shortage of responses.

> "I see the blood of Jesus painted on the door's threshold."
> "It looks like a place of peace in the storm."
> "I see a cross."
> "Is that a red "5" right there? That's the number of grace."
> "I think it's an invitation to enter God's Presence."

Among all this interaction my attention was drawn to a middle-age woman with short-cropped hair and a countenance of sadness about her. Joining the discussion, she moved right up close to the canvas and gestured with her hands as she counted the vertical white strokes. "Eleven," she said out loud. Then putting her face right up next to the canvas she used her finger to count the small vertical red strokes. Once again she said, "Eleven."

"I know what you painted!" she said with a touch of gentle excitement in her voice as she turned from the canvas. We all waited for her to continue. "It's the eleventh hour. God is bringing time to a close, and we're in the eleventh hour."

I sensed a bit of awe fall upon us all as I remembered:

I'm disclosing myself in the fullness of time.

Her name was Lillie, and she lingered to talk with me as the folks around us began to disperse. As she shared her story with me, I felt her sadness return - only I learned it was not sadness, but grief. Her husband joined us as she explained that they were living in the aftermath of their only son's death from a heroin overdose. Although overwhelmed by grief and unshakable depression, their faith seemed grounded.

"We came for prayer tonight - partly for my depression, but mostly for my fibromyalgia." My heart was drawn toward her with overwhelming compassion. I felt the Lord's compassion, too, for her brokenness. But I also felt his hope for her.

Give her the painting.

Rats! I was hoping he wouldn't say that because I really wanted to keep this painting for my own collection. "Do I have to, Lord? I love this one."

I know. Give her the painting.

In obedience, I gifted the painting to her. Initially, she refused, "Oh no. It's too much. We can't."

Laughing gently in response, I explained, "You have to take it because the Holy Spirit just told me that I couldn't keep it. He wants you to have it."

Joyful tears rolled down Lillie's face as she tried to explain, "But it's too big for our car."

After assuring her that I would be happy to deliver it to their home, I felt the Holy Spirit's further prompting as I shared about my own struggle with depression and told briefly of my supernatural healing. I could tell that I had made a connection with her. I further explained to her that the painting has no mystical or miraculous power in and of itself. "But put it where you can see it often. Every time you stop to look at it, I encourage you to remember my story and thank God for being your healer, too."

With the painting delivered the following week I thought little more about it until about six weeks later when I discovered an unexpected letter in my mail box. I didn't recognize the return address but opened it with curiosity. It was from Lillie. She reminded me of the painting and told how she did just what I encouraged her to do.

Her written words were uplifting and optimistic with no hint of depression as she thanked me for the painting, "It hangs on the wall right next to my bed and I am absolutely so blessed by it every day. My husband and I are being set free, and I believe my fibromyalgia is gone!"

Now that's a true, snail-mail blessing! I did my own happy dance to celebrate.

IN JOY!

"THE ANOINTING"

     I love this painting as one of my all-time favorites. It's one that flowed out of me so freely, and I knew exactly what it meant - or so I thought.

     I painted the version on the left - an upward release of praise and worship. I saw it clearly in my mind's eye during worship. It was simple, yet powerful. The "praise" itself was painted in iridescent colors - quite striking against the rich blue background. It was joyful. Folks in the room around me seemed to catch the joy, too, as they commented on its uplifting spirit.

     Then I noticed one of the healing team leaders standing off at a distance. He was focused on the painting with an intent look on his face. Eventually, he approached the easel, reached up, turned the painting upside down, and set it back on the easel. "This is a picture of your anointing," he stated matter-of-factly. I heard laughter rise up in my spirit as I delightfully thought, "Jehovah Sneaky, is that you?"

     I had just painted my own prophetic encouragement without even knowing it!

IMPASSIONED STORIES

"BREAKING DOWN STRONGHOLDS"

In response to my question, "Holy Spirit, what do you want to paint tonight?" I felt his response in my spirit: *I'm breaking down strongholds*. I spent a few more minutes in worship and then got up to paint.

I began by painting a background of varying hues of bluish gray from light to dark across the horizontal canvas. The strokes were free, random, and overlapping within this dark-to-light motif. Then, to represent the "strongholds," I began to paint repeating, randomly-spaced vertical lines on the right side of the canvas.

As I began to form these vertical "bars" I was distracted by a particular stroke of white paint I had made on the left side of the canvas. It wasn't properly blending into the background. I was making a move to correct the "problem" when I felt the Holy Spirit say urgently, "Stop." At that same moment a young woman came rushing toward me with a sense of urgency.

"I had to come up close to see the doves!!" She exclaimed, "They're so beautiful! I could see them from way back there." I was startled. *Doves?* I remained silent as she directed her attention to the painting. Almost immediately she looked back at me. "Oh," she said, obviously disappointed, "They're not there. I'm so sorry." She explained with embarrassment, "From back there I thought I saw doves."

"You did!" I exclaimed even though I could not see the doves myself.

Confusion washed over her face as she looked again at the painting, then back at me. I explained, "The Holy Spirit opened the spirit realm tonight so you could see doves. If he allowed you to see them, they are there!" Her face brightened up.

We talked for a few moments, and I learned that her name was Rosie. "What are these?" she asked, pointing to the vertical bars.

"Those are strongholds." I could tell that she was not familiar with the term, so I began to explain that strongholds are lies that we believe about ourselves or about God that are contrary to God's Truth. "We believe those lies," I explained, "and they prevent us from experiencing the freedom Christ wants us to have. For most of my life I believed the lie, 'I'm unlovable.' Of course it was a lie, but I couldn't see it. Unknowingly, I allowed it to become a major barrier to how I saw myself and how I interacted with the people around me."

I directed her attention back to my painting, "See this bar out here by itself? That's the 'I'm unlovable' stronghold. I believed that lie, and I kept it out there in front of me to keep people at a distance. All these other bars? Those are all lies, too: 'Nobody really likes you. Everyone will eventual reject you. God only loves you because he has to.'" I further explained that although it made me feel safe, it was really just a prison of lies that kept me from experiencing God's pure love.

I continued, "Once I opened myself up to receiving God's Truth about me, he began to tear down those strongholds and replace them with his love." Looking directly at her I said, "I sense that God wants to break through a lie that you're believing about yourself."

She protested gently, "Oh. I'm not here to be prayed for. I just brought my friends who needed a ride."

"That's fine," I said. "But keep your heart open, because God allowed you to see into the spirit realm tonight for a reason." I told her that it would be about thirty minutes before the painting was finished. "Will you still be here?" She nodded affirmatively. "Good. Come back then because I want you to have this painting." A huge smile spread across her face as she assured me that she would return.

I began to pray earnestly for her as she walked away, returning my focus to the painting. I felt in my spirit that God was up to something! Trust me when I say that, even though I couldn't see them myself, I was not about to paint over her doves! I completed the painting with one final, dramatic element: a horizontal line of energetic movement, cutting through the stronghold bars and shattering them along its path. It was really fun to paint that part because I could feel the Holy Spirit's pleasure as I did.

When Rosie returned she looked a mess! But a beautiful one. Her face was aglow with joy and excitement. Tears were running down her face as she unashamedly declared, "You were right. I was believing a lie! The lady prayed with me about it, and then I received the Baptism of the Holy Spirit! I can't believe it! Just now! She prayed for me, and I received the Holy Spirit!"

I saw pure joy in the eyes of that young woman. As she turned to leave with my painting in her hands and, with her friends at her side, she bounced out a little happy dance and said, "I'm sooo happy!!"

Yep. Strongholds were broken, indeed.

Afterwards, I scrutinized the photograph of that painting to see if I could "see" the doves. It took two days, but there it was – positioned on the left-hand side of the painting like a bird on a wire. There is also another one, positioned in flight, in the bottom left-hand corner.

I did not, nor *could* not, see the doves when I added that bold stroke of color across the middle of the canvas. In fact, I could have painted it right through either one of the doves. But instead, the Holy Spirit directed me to paint it as a resting place for his dove.

Do you see the Spirit-empowering truth here? God's peace rests on the release of his power.

IN JOY!

"HEAVEN'S DOOR"

"That's the door of heaven!" he exclaimed with vibrant enthusiasm. I turned around to see three young boys standing behind me, all stair-stepped in height and hovered around their mom. I asked, "Who sees heaven's door?"

Not the tallest of the bunch, I guessed him to be about ten years old as he exuberantly declared, "I do!"

I caught his mom's eye as I asked him to tell me his name.

"I'm Darius," he said matter-of-factly.

"Well, Darius," I asked, "How big is heaven's door?" He hesitated.

I continued, "I'm going to keep painting, Darius, but I want you think about how big heaven's door really is." He seemed excited by the challenge, and his brothers joined in, too.

At this point of the painting's completion I had yet to add the central figure. (Put your finger on the picture above, just over the tiny figure in the middle of the light rays, and you'll get a sense of what they were seeing when I posed the question.)

The boys were throwing out guesses as I continued to paint: "Ten inches." Then one of the other brothers would chime in, "No. Twelve inches?" To which I replied, "I think heaven's door is bigger than that. Don't you?"

Then with the cunning of a ten-year-old Darius asked nonchalantly, "How tall is that canvas?" I grinned to myself, enjoying this game as much as they were. But their minds were focused on earth-bound reality - the actual height of a canvas. I decided to shift their focus,

"How tall are you, Darius?"

He responded with a confused look on his face. I teased him with another question, "Do you think heaven's door is bigger than you?" He hesitated before responding with less assurance in his voice, "Probably."

"How much bigger?" I volleyed back. His brothers remained silent in an apparent effort to let Darius take the fall.

He shrugged his shoulders in response.

"Do you want to see how big heaven's door is?"

His eyes perked up. "How about, y'all?" I said as I caught the eyes of his brothers. They nodded, too.

"OK," I said. "Gather round so you can see the canvas, and I'll show you how big heaven's door really is. Are you ready?" I saw looks of anticipation in response. I turned back to the canvas.

With three tiny brush strokes the central figure came to life, and I heard the boys respond in unison, "Woah!"

Darius looked up at me with delight and revelation dancing in his eyes. "That's really big!" He looked at his mom seeking confirmation, and we all had a good laugh in response.

It's simply a matter of perspective!

"WORSHIP RISING"

In response to my question, "What do you want to paint tonight, Lord?" I saw in my mind's eye a wall of flowing water - a fountain where you can't see the release of the water but only ripples flowing down the wall.

The top image shown here is the original orientation of the painting. I applied a lot of water to the application of the blue paint, allowing it to flow easily and drip freely. As I stepped back for a moment I received further direction:

Add a thin, dark line about two-thirds up. Start at the left.

OK, now stop. Add some color.

I asked for further clarification in my spirit, "What colors?"

You decide.

Normally when given the choice I choose purple, but that night, I felt that some vibrant, warm colors would be a nice contrast among the flow of blue. I played around with strokes of varying styles - bold verticals, flowing drips, and a stack of short staccato horizontal lines.

I stepped back from the canvas, "What next, Lord?

Do it again - only higher.

I wasn't exactly sure what that meant but I repeated the dark horizontal line in the upper right-hand corner of the canvas. I added some additional color but kept it tight and confined. I waited again.

Part the blue between.

"Between what?" My request for clarification hung unanswered. The blue paint was completely dry, so I wasn't sure how to "part" it. Eventually, I added an upward stroke of white paint, "parting the blue between" the upper and lower vertical lines. I liked it. It felt good. Satisfying.

It's upside down.

"Really?" I thought to myself. I removed the canvas from the easel and, after reorienting it, stepped back to view it. I was surprised by the change. The downward flow had been transformed into uplifting momentum. It felt more powerful and dynamic. I pondered the image with inquiry, "Lord, what are you saying to me through this painting?" Clearly, I heard in my spirit:

I'm calling you up to a higher place of worship.

I felt the precious weight of holiness settle over me.

IN JOY!

"STANDING ON HIS PROMISES"

"What is the Holy Spirit calling you to paint tonight?" my fellow artist Victoria asked as we went about setting up our easels. I raised my hands in a gesture of praise which she mistakenly interpreted as a shrug of uncertainty. Always an encourager, she said, "I'm sure he'll give you something as you get started."

"No," I clarified. "I'm supposed to paint this." I raised my hands again in an outstretched, upward gesture. She laughed in response.

I wasn't sure exactly how to put that motion onto the canvas. I felt I needed to capture not just the gesture itself but the upward motion - the momentum of moving upward. I began painting in the background with lots of white, butter yellow and blue greys. It felt on some level like I was stalling because I was unsure how to capture the essence of the gesture I'd seen.

Several people were making comments about how peaceful and tranquil the painting looked - which was not at all what I was trying to capture. "Lord, how do I transform it from here?" I listened. No response. I waited. Suddenly, I felt the need for red.

Because I would never have thought to put such a bold color onto the neutral background before me, I knew it was a "God thought." Just as I had finished preparing my palette with a bold array of red paint, my friend Abigail commented from behind me, "Wow! I love what you've done so far. But those are not your usual colors, at all." When I turned to speak with her, I realized that she was talking about the painting, not my palette. "Yes," I replied as I turned to reveal my palette, "but I'm supposed to add this." She smiled knowingly, "Does that make you a little nervous?" To my affirmative head nod, she quipped pleasantly, "Then it must be God!"

I smiled in my spirit as I turned back toward the canvas, prayed for confidence, and then boldly began to release that red color with abandon. It felt good. I focused on the *feeling* of upward momentum and introduced the central character so quickly that I didn't really have time to give it any detailed thought. I stepped back to take in the results with amazement.

Now, all hesitation was gone. I began to accentuate the feeling of movement in the painting by adding accent strokes of color under her arms. As I did, I began to "feel" wind sweep across the painting. I accentuated her hair with motion as this painting came alive with energy and power. I struggle to explain it with words, but I sensed in those moments that I was capturing on canvas a breakthrough in the spirit realm. But there was nothing on the canvas above the momentum of her gesture.

I don't recall asking the Holy Spirit for direction as to how to fill the

upper third of the canvas. I just felt like I was to fill it with joy. And joy, to me, is always represented by lots of color. And so I was about the business of filling in the "heavens" with joy when a woman approached and commented about the feeling of power in the painting.

    As I turned to talk with her I saw emotion in her face and tear-stained eyes - not in response to the painting, but in response to the emotion of her circumstances. Her name was Janice, and she told me that her husband was dealing with leukemia. But she did not speak out of despair. She spoke out of faith, "We're asking God for healing, but we're looking at our situation as a new mission field. During the last round of chemotherapy, we had the opportunity to share our faith with one of the nurses, and she gave her life to Christ." She smiled in response to the memory as I heard the Holy Spirit speak clearly to my spirit:

You just painted her.

(Now that's just cool!)

Janice's husband, Randy, approached as I began to encourage her. "This is you." I told her, gesturing to the painting. "You are a prayer warrior. You are standing on God's promises and walking in his power. Your circumstances will not control you. Nor will your situation overwhelm you. You are strong. You are grounded, and the momentum of your prayers will fill the heavens with joy."

Tears welled up again in her eyes. Randy smiled and said both enthusiastically and with admiration in his voice, "That's exactly who she is."

I introduced myself to him and then felt led to encourage him with a brief version of my own healing testimony and some words of optimism. I then invited them to wait while I finished up the painting because I wanted them to have it. They readily agreed as several other folks came over to see and comment. Once it was finished, photographed, and signed, I handed it over to them.

As Randy reached out to receive it from me he asked if he could share with me what he felt the Holy Spirit was telling him as he watched me finish up the painting.

"Sure!" I responded without hesitation as he began.

"You painted a self-portrait. This is a picture of who you are. You are an intercessor. A prayer warrior, too. You feel and release joy when you pray, but that's not what you painted. What you painted was the opening up of the heavens that happens when you pray and call down heaven to earth. And all those colorful dots? Those are the faces of all the people you lift up before the Father's throne. You encourage them. You lift them up. And that one right there?" His voice choked with emotion. "The dark purple one?" he said as he pointed to one "face" in particular (directly above her head and just below the top of the canvas.) "That's me. Thank you for encouraging me with your story and praying for me."

Hugs and tears all around! Another canvas had found its rightful home. As I watched them leave hand-in-hand I sensed in my spirit that all would be well with them. I knew it would be with me.

"HEALING SWOOSH"

As I began this painting, I received no discernable answer to my question, "Holy Spirit, what do you want to paint tonight?" But I had a strong sense that yellow-gold was my starting point. As I began to lay in the colors and allow them to flow freely, I saw a pathway emerge.

It led to an empty space on the canvas that I enhanced with strong, textural white. Was it a pathway of obstacles leading to a light source? Was it the torn veil of the temple allowing access to God's throne room? It felt like a holy place, and as the image took shape I found myself wondering what it would be like to step into this painting. What would it sound like? Smell like? Feel like? I had a sense that it would smell sweet and feel holy.

As I was contemplating the painting in this light, I heard in my spirit: *Add a swoosh!*

I wasn't sure exactly what a "swoosh" meant, but I felt that it should be bold and dramatic. However, I was so enjoying this flowing, golden environment that I hesitated to ruin it by a potentially misplaced "swoosh." The response I heard in my spirit when I asked the Holy Spirit for direction about placement and color was not helpful at all.

You decide.

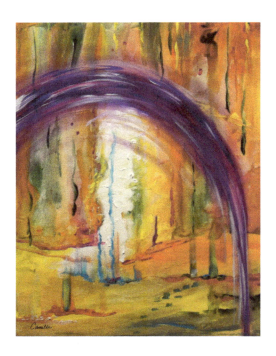

When in doubt, I always choose purple. I was preparing my palette with purple paint when Emily, one of the healing team members, came up and asked, "What is this painting all about?" I explained my process and indicated the bold purple paint on my palette. "I'm supposed to add a purple swoosh. It's hard to describe," I continued, "But it feels holy. I have no idea why, but what I'm about to paint feels holy."

Sensing my hesitation, she encouraged me. "You paint while I stand here and pray." She stood next to the canvas facing me with an encouraging "you-can-do-it" expression on her face. I needed it because painting this swoosh was beginning to feel like a weighty responsibility.

Unaware that a small group of people had gathered directly behind me, I loaded my brush with purple paint and began my bold "swoosh." As soon as the brush hit the canvas, I heard a woman gasp behind me. Literally! I stayed focused on the task at hand but was keenly aware of the voices behind me. Two women were speaking Spanish in an animated fashion.

Having completed my fast-and-furious "swoosh," I laid down my brush and turned around to see a young, Hispanic woman with tears rolling down her cheeks. Apparently she spoke little-to-no English and was encouraging her older friend to try to tell me what was happening. Through their choppy English and excited tears I learned that they were both visiting from Florida and had come to my church to observe how we operate our Healing Rooms. The younger of the two had also requested prayer for a medical condition that, as best as I could make out, was some form of cancer.

They were both so excited and both trying their best to tell me their story without the aid of an interpreter. But they made it clear that they wanted me to understand what was happening. Apparently, before I added the purple swoosh, my painting looked, to her, like the image of her cancer – maybe an MRI or cell image of some sort. The younger woman made a motion with her hands to imitate the "swoosh" motion and exclaimed, "It gone! No sick!" After a bit more excited Spanish exchange between them, her friend said, "She see her sickness in your picture. But you make (she indicted the swoosh motion) and her sickness go away! Her pain is no more."

We didn't need further language to celebrate her healing. All we needed were tears and hugs. Now, I don't know if her cancer was brushed away by my prophetic "swoosh," but what I do know is that God used my obedience in that moment to release His power into her circumstances. He spoke to her heart through a painting and revealed to her that she had been healed. She felt it. She gave God the glory for it. And she left Texas with a painting in her hand as a remembrance of her encounter with Jesus, her healer.

"NEW BEGINNINGS"

I was finishing up the leaves on this painting when a blonde woman caught my eye. I saw her coming across the room as if she were making her way straight to me. She was. She introduced herself as she dabbed her tear-stained eyes and asked, "May I tell you something about your painting?"

With my consent she told of how she had been sitting in the worship center behind me as she waited for her turn with the prayer team. "As I watched you paint in that bold red color I got angry. I mean really angry. I had no idea why." After a moment of hesitation, she warily confessed, "I'm a surviving victim

of long-term sexual abuse and maybe that red color just sparked a nerve. But I was so angry at you for painting it that I got up to leave. Just as I did, a woman on the healing team told me it was my turn for prayer, so I went with her instead of leaving. And I'm so glad I did."

She then told of how that woman had prayed for her physical healing but then began to speak prophetically about how God was healing her emotions, too - how He was going to restore her joy and bring new life into her heart.

"I felt something melt in my heart as she prayed, and I felt peace." Her face brightened further as she recalled, "And as I turned around to leave, I looked back at your painting. By that time you had painted all these leaves. God spoke to my heart and told me that he is releasing "new life" over my anger and abuse. I saw it! In your painting - I saw it!"

We celebrated together as I thanked her for sharing her story with me. "Can you wait just a moment?" I asked. We made small talk as I completed a few final brush strokes, photographed the painting, and signed my name to it. Then removing it from the easel, I handed it to her and said, "Be careful with it for a bit until it dries."

Delight washed over her face. (That's my favorite part of prophetic painting.) She hugged and thanked me, and I watched her leave, painting in hand. But she didn't make it very far. In fact, I saw her talking to several different folks during the time it took me to clean up my paint area and pack things away. Each encounter was animated by her enthusiastic gestures toward the painting as she apparently told the story of her divinely-orchestrated evening. Joy rose in my heart as I contemplated the ripple effect of Spirit-empowered living.

"WINDOW IN THE NIGHT"

I love to enter into worship before I paint prophetically, and I always ask the Holy Spirit the same question, "What do you want to paint tonight?" Sometimes I get a word or phrase upon which to build a painting. At other times, I see an image in my mind's eye or have a strong leaning toward one color or another.

On this particular evening, while worshiping in the Healing Rooms, I heard the phrase

Window in the Night pop into my mind. I pondered the phrase, asking the Lord for further insight. In my mind's eye I saw a starry night sky and the frame of a foggy, or dirty, window pane – *a window in the night*. I could see the window pane, but I couldn't see through it.

I began painting the outer border with a night sky, but there didn't seem much value in painting a clouded-over window pane. As soon as I asked the Holy Spirit, "What's behind the window pane?" he brought to my remembrance a Scripture reference from 1 Corinthians 13:12a:

"For now we see in a mirror dimly, but then face to face."

As I pondered this verse with my mind's eye, the cloudy window pane faded and clarity flooded in. What emerged at the end of my paint brush was a delightful environment of color and joy. In it was movement, light, energy and life. The contrast between the cloudy window pane in my mind's eye and this life-affirming image could not have been more vivid. And it occurred to me in that moment that this is what a relationship with the Holy Spirit is all about. Cloudy things become bright. Confusion gives way to focus. And things that previously made no sense become clear.

I was thoroughly enjoying my moment of revelation when my dear friend and fellow-painter, Victoria, came up and inquired about what the Lord was saying to me.

"I keep hearing the phrase 'window in the night'," I replied, "and I'm still trying to determine exactly what that means."

"I know what it means!" she responded cheerfully and then immediately walked away to attend to another task. In her wake I pondered further. I understood cloudy things becoming bright, but what was the significance of the night setting?

She returned shortly to rescue me from my pondering. "Windows in the night are the prophetic dreams God gives us while we sleep."

Profound, yet simple. I love that about God!

"KEYHOLE GLORY"

I was sitting in my car in the church parking lot, having just finished my fast-food fare, when an image popped into my mind's eye. Actually it was more of a pattern than an image – repetitive stripes of red and black. "That's interesting," I mused to myself as I popped the trunk and got out to unload my art supplies.

Throughout worship that night I kept seeing that same pattern. It was like a wall of red and black stripes - only the stripes had movement in them. And then I noticed a pin-prick of light. In my mind's eye I zoomed in closer to see if I could identify the light source. It turned out to be a keyhole, and I felt in my spirit:

Paint that.

So I approached my canvas that night with red and black paint. At first it felt good to fill the white space of the canvas with such bold and contrasting colors. But then it began to feel heavy. About that time one of the other artists interrupted my thoughts with an enthusiastic opinion, "It looks so joyful!"

Joyful? I didn't get that at all. It had taken on a dark, oppressive feel to me. I continued to paint, trusting that eventually the keyhole would make it feel lighter.

With the stripes completed I fully intended to paint a more traditional image of a keyhole. I envisioned an interior scene on the other side of the "door" – similar to my painting "Window in the Night". But in my mind's eye, as I peered into the keyhole, I was surprised by glory. It came rushing forward and spilling out all over and around me. I tried to capture that in the painting.

But after the "keyhole" (glory and all) was set in place among the striped background, it still felt oppressive to me. It was not until I added the expanding, concentric circles that I felt the oppression lift.

"It's a bride." I heard someone comment. A question followed, "Is it an angel?"

Honestly, I had no interpretation at the time other than to say that I felt that somehow oppression had been swept away by glory. It was not until a few weeks later that the Lord interpreted it more personally for me.

My friend, Laurie, stopped by my house for a visit and was drawn to "Keyhole Glory" as it stood propped up on my mantle. She asked a simple question followed by an intriguing comment: "Is this a new painting? It reminds me of what you've just been through."

I was startled that she had connected my circumstances with the painting. I had, indeed, just come out of a season of situational uncertainty. Although it has been a challenging time in my life's journey, I stood on the promises of God and deliberately choose faith over fear.

"When you were in that scary place," she continued, "you didn't give in to the fear. You told me that you stood there and sang because that's all you knew to do. You refused to believe the negativity that was being spoken over you, and you stood there in faith and sang. Don't you think this painting looks like that?"

It had not occurred to me until then, but I sensed that she was right.

"By that act of faith," she encouraged, "You denied the enemy and tapped into God as your power source. You brought him into the situation with you and trusted that he would release his power and fight the fight for you. And he did!"

She was right about that. God had intervened and my season of testing had ended in victory. Oppression had, indeed, been swept away in the wake of God's glory!

"And," Laurie reminded me with a teasing grin in her voice, "not only did you bring down God's glory, you left a trail of it behind you!"

"LIQUID LOVE"

It was an empty bowl. I saw it clearly in my mind's eye during worship. Just a simple, plain, empty bowl. "Why are you showing me an empty bowl, Lord?" No answer. I remained in worship for another twenty or thirty minutes trying to make sense of why the Lord would want me to paint an empty bowl. Eventually, I conceded, "OK, Lord. An empty bowl it is."

Just as I was about to rise, I saw an explosion of color being poured into that empty bowl. It came from a source I could not see, hitting the bowl like a target and splashing around its interior. Had this occurred in the natural world, those colors would have mixed into a pool of lifeless brown muck. But here in my mind's eye the colors danced around together while maintaining their original hues. Something else struck me as odd as I continued to see the movie-like image being played out in my mind's eye. The color continued to flow from its original source but the bowl never filled up or reached its capacity to receive the continuous flow of color.

"That's so cool, Lord. What is it?" The question hung there unanswered as I headed toward my canvas to see if I could capture what I had just seen.

I sensed that a neutral background would set the stage for a contrast of color and painted it in quickly. I added the empty bowl. Then I hesitated. I was not sure I could adequately capture what I had seen in my mind's eye. How would

I keep the colors from becoming a muddy mess? In a procrastinating attempt to delay the challenge, I took a restful break. "Time to clean my brushes a bit," I rationalized.

Upon my return, I turned the corner and saw one of my fellow artists, Abigail, standing directly in front of the painting. I made a flippantly humorous comment as I approached and regretted it almost immediately. The Holy Spirit was speaking to her through the painting, and I had disrespectfully interrupted.

"That's how I feel." she

explained, having not seemed to take any offense at my interruption. "I feel empty. I'm that empty vessel." Respectfully, I encouraged her to wait until the painting was complete to see its transformation.

As she walked away I felt even more pressure. Looking down at my palette I thought to myself, "How do I add all this color without making a mess of it?" Immediately I felt and heard a correction in my spirit:

Who's creating this painting? You or me?

Ouch! "Forgive me, Lord. You are."

Then relax and have fun with it.

I do not know how I painted this painting. The release of color came out fast and clear. The paint seemed to supernaturally stay in place without blending into mud or losing its clarity. It seemed to dry at super-fast speed. Ironically, it dried so quickly, that I had to spray it with water to make the paint run for artistic effect. I then added a shadow under the bowl to ground it and some reflective color in the foreground for cohesiveness.

Stepping back from the painting with a sense of wonderment, I celebrated in my spirit, "That was fun, Lord!" I added some defining strokes to make sure the outline of the glass bowl would remain visible and posed an awestruck question, "Lord, how did you do that?"

Before I could get an answer I realized that Abigail was standing behind me. She no longer had defeat in her voice. She had wonderment. "That's amazing," she said. "It was an empty bowl. Then it was a swirl of color. Now I can see the bowl again with the color swirling around inside of it. How did you do that?"

Without waiting for a response she changed the subject by asking, "Did you take a picture of it before you added the color?" When I replied that I had not, she seemed disappointed. "That empty bowl really touched me. It spoke to how I've been feeling lately." Immediately, I felt the Holy Spirit's prompting:

Tell her I'm filling her empty bowl with my liquid love.

(Awesome, right?)

"FALLING INTO GRACE"

Freedom in Christ is an on-going process, and sometimes life demands that we pause and ask ourselves, "Am I truly free in this area of my life?" More often than not, the area of bondage is exposed by the words or actions of another person. The resulting pain can feel unbearable, but we have a choice to make.

Recently, I was the recipient of some harshly-delivered words. They were personal, judgmental, unfair, and deeply-wounding to my spirit. I retreated. I cried - a lot. I began to build a wall of resistance and unforgiveness toward this person, and I was miserable.

One afternoon while trying to rationalize to the Lord all the resentment I'd been carrying around for weeks, I heard his gentle prompting - *Let go*. I didn't want to let go. I was justified. I had been the victim. With tender relentlessness he pursued me: *Let go. Just let go.*

My stubborn resistance eventually gave way to God's welcoming grace, and I confessed my unforgiveness, acknowledging Jesus as Lord over my woundedness. Immediately, in my mind's eye, I saw and felt myself falling. I was falling in slow motion from what seemed like a vast height, but I had no fear. I had simply let go. I had no idea what awaited me upon "impact," but I was free in the descent and fear had no place. All I felt in the experience was peaceful release.

I felt prompted to paint the experience during public worship the following Sunday, but beyond a small silhouette on a blank canvas I had no vision. Once in place, however, the silhouette lost its significance among the color that began to splash around inside my mind's eye. I excitedly filled my palette and flowed onto the canvas an array of joyful colors. It was quick and effortless. As I stepped back to view the finished piece, I felt such joy. *Now,* I could finally see the grace into which I had fallen.

"BROKEN VESSEL FILLED WITH LIVING WATER"

This is the watercolor image I described in Chapter 1. I painted and completed it just a day or two before the 2009 January Dallas Gift Market where I met Lee. I had been thinking about creating this painting for several months before the upcoming show that year, but I struggled to find time to put in on paper. As the Market dates drew closer I had a sense of urgency, feeling in my spirit that it had to get it done before Market.

Somehow I worked it in among all my other preparations without understanding why it seemed so pressing. It was not until I met Lee and heard him describe this painting to me in such prophetic detail that I came to understand why I had such a sense of urgency to finish it before Market. It was to be a significant point of connection.

At the time, Lee's ability to describe it (unseen) really freaked me out. In hindsight, it confirmed that God had undoubtedly orchestrated it all.

During our time together at that four-day trade show, God released a lot of prophetic words to me through Lee – words of knowledge that were insightful and deeply personal, many of which were too personal to share in this public forum. But the sheer intimacy of them testified of their authenticity and to the rich, personal nature of God.

IN JOY!

"ME AND LEE"

I told you all about my healing story in the first few chapters of this book, describing how God used Lee as a spiritual game-changer in my life. Now, I want to introduce you to him.

"Everyone, meet Lee. Lee, meet everyone!"

This photograph of me and Lee was taken on "Celebration Sunday" four days after my healing. The photographic quality is less than ideal, but I love this photograph. I love the memory of this captured moment. And I love this Spirit-empowered man.

Lee and I have maintained a rich friendship over the intervening years, and it's a joy to have him in my life. He continues to speak prophetic wisdom into my life and encourages me to become in the Spirit all I was designed to be.

"Thank you, Lee, for being faithful to the call. You are so very dear to me."

RESOURCES

The following is a list of resources that have been significant guides in my quest to understand and experience Spirt-empowered living. It is by no means an exhaustive list of the subject matter, but in my collection these are belovedly dog-eared:

FREEDOM & DELIVERANCE:

Bob Hamp, *Think Differently Live Differently* (USA, Thinking Differently Press, 2010)

Don Dickerman, *When Pigs Move In* (Lake Mary, FL: Charisma House, 2009).

Robert Morris, *Truly Free* (Nashville, TN: Thomas Nelson, 2015)

WORSHIP & PRAYER:

Dutch Sheets, *Intercessory Prayer* (Ventura, CA: Regal Books, a division of Gospel Light, 1996)

Zach Neese, *How to Worship a King* (USA: Gateway Create, 2012)

PROPHESY & SPIRT-EMPOWERED LIVING:

Bill Johnson, *When Heaven Invades Earth* (Shippensburg, PA: Treasure House, an imprint of Destiny Image Publishers, Inc., 2003)

Graham Cooke, *Approaching the Heart of Prophecy* (Vacaville, CA: Brilliant Book House LLC, 2006)

Graham Cooke, *Prophetic Wisdom* (Vacaville, CA: Brilliant Book House LLC, 2010)

Graham Cooke, "Art of Thinking Brilliantly," audio series (Brilliant Book House, 2013), compact disk.

IN JOY!

Graham Cooke, "Mind of a Saint" audio series (Brilliant Book House, 2013) compact disk.

John G. Lake, His Life, His Sermons, His Boldness of Faith (Fort Worth, TX: Kenneth Copeland Publications, 1994)

Robert Morris, *Frequency* (Nashville, TN: W Publishing Group, an imprint of Thomas Nelson, 2016)

Robert Morris, *The God I Never Knew* (Waterbrook Press, 2011)

FINANCIAL FREEDOM:

Robert Morris, *The Blessed Life* (Bethany House Publishers, revised, updated ed.edition, 2016)

Shawn Bolz, *Keys to Heaven's Economy* (Glendale, CA: ICreate Productions, 2015)

END NOTES

[1] Transcutaneous Electrical Nerve Stimulation (TENS) – a medical device that uses electric current to stimulate nerves for the purpose of pain management.

[2] Evangelical Protestantism is the movement within Protestant Christianity that identifies the essence of the gospel message as the doctrine of salvation by grace through faith in the redemptive work of Jesus Christ's death and resurrection.

[3] 1 Corinthians 12:8-10.

[4] In Christianity, cessationism is the doctrine that spiritual gifts such as speaking in tongues, prophecy and healing ceased after the death of the original twelve apostles.

[5] Romans 8:28 (paraphrased).

[6] Isaiah 55:9 (paraphrased).

[7] 1 Timothy 6:12 (paraphrased).

[8] Pentecostalism places special emphasis on a direct personal experience of God through the baptism with the Holy Spirit.

[9] 2 Corinthians 5:17, ESV.

[10] *Ibid.*

[11] 1 John 4:16; Psalm 103:8; Psalm 86:5; Titus 2:11; 1 Chronicles 28:20.

[12] Marcus M Wells (1815-1895). "Holy Spirit, Faithful Guide," in *Baptist Hymnal*, 20th ed., ed. Walter Hines Sims, 165, Nashville: Convention Press, 1956.

[13] Isaac Watts (1674-1748). "Am I a Soldier of the Cross," in *Baptist Hymnal*, 20th ed., ed. Walter Hines Sims, 405, Nashville: Convention Press, 1956.

[14] Charles H Gabriel (1856-1932). "I Stand Amazed in the Presence," in *Baptist Hymnal*, 20th ed., ed. Walter Hines Sims, 139, Nashville: Convention Press, 1956.

[15] Jessie Brown Pounds (1861-1921). "I Know that My Redeemer Liveth," in *Baptist Hymnal*, 20th ed., ed. Walter Hines Sims, 127, Nashville: Convention Press, 1956.

[16] George Bennard (1873-1958). "The Old Rugged Cross," in *Baptist Hymnal*, 20th ed., ed. Walter Hines Sims, 93, Nashville: Convention Press, 1956.

[17] William Cowper (1731-1800). "There is a Fountain," in *Baptist Hymnal*, 20th ed., ed. Walter Hines Sims, 92, Nashville: Convention Press, 1956.

[18] Fanny J Crosby (1820-1915). "I Am thine, O Lord," in *Baptist Hymnal*, 20th ed., ed. Walter Hines Sims, 349, Nashville: Convention Press, 1956.

[19] Luke 14:27 (paraphrased).

IN JOY!

[20] Psalm 22:3 (paraphrased).

[21] Psalm 100:4 (paraphrased).

[22] 2 Corinthians 3:17 (paraphrased).

[23] Psalm 16:11 (paraphrased).

[24] Bennard, *op. cit.*

[25] John 2:15, ESV (parenthetical insight added).

[26] Exodus 25:17-22.

[27] I Corinthians 3:16.

[28] Don Dickerman, *When Pigs Move In* (Lake Mary, FL: Charisma House, 2009).

[29] Don Dickerman, *ibid.*, 46.

[30] Personal note: Billy called the demon by name, but I will not honor a demon by acknowledging his name in print.

[31] 2 Chronicles 29:35, AMP (paraphrased).

[32] John 10:10, ESV.

[33] Isaiah 61:1 (paraphrased).

[34] John 8:32, ESV (paraphrased with parenthetical insight added).

[35] Proverbs 18:21, ESV.

[36] This is a colloquial phrase used often by Don Dickerman in his public speaking and newsletters.

[37] 2 Corinthians 12:2, ESV.

[38] John 15:5, ESV.

[39] Genesis 3:8, ESV.

[40] Genesis 2:17 (paraphrased.)

[41] Bob Hamp, *Think Differently Live Differently* (USA, Thinking Differently Press, 2010), 87.

[42] Hebrews 4:16 (paraphrased).

[43] Philippians 4:6 (paraphrased).

[44] Acts 2.

END NOTES

[45] The word "*Selah*," used over seventy times in the Psalms, has an unknown meaning. It is thought to be a reminder to stop and reflect in stillness upon the meaning of what you've just read.

[46] General reference to Robert Morris, *The God I Never Knew* (Waterbrook Press, 2011).

[47] Kim Walker. *Here is My Song*. Jesus Culture Music, 2008, compact disc.

[48] Ephesians 1:19, NIV.

[49] Genesis 1:1, ESV.

[50] Matthew 3:2, ESV.

[51] 2 Corinthians 5:17.

[52] Matthew 5:21, 27, 31, 33, 38, 43.

[53] *Chariots of Fire*. Directed by Hugh Hudson, 20th Century Fox, 1981.

[54] Psalm 102: 18, NIV and 2 Corinthians 5:17, ESV.

[55] Luke 14:27 (paraphrased).

[56] Hebrew 12:2.